EAS

History

Hugo Frey

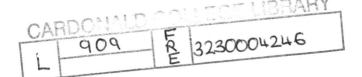

TEACH YOURSELF BOOKS

For UK orders: please contact Bookpoint Ltd, 130 Milton Park, Abingdon, Oxon OX14 4SB. Telephone: (44) 01235 827720. Fax: (44) 01235 400454. Lines are open from 9.00–6.00, Monday to Saturday, with a 24-hour message answering service. Email address: orders@bookpoint.co.uk

For U.S.A. order enquiries: please contact McGraw-Hill Customer Services, P.O. Box 545, Blacklick, OH 43004-0545, U.S.A. Telephone: 1-800-722-4728. Fax: 1-614-755-5645.

For Canada order enquiries: please contact McGraw-Hill Ryerson Ld., 300 Water St, Whitby, Ontario L1N 9B6, Canada. Telephone: 905 430 5000. Fax: 905 430 5020.

Long renowned as the authoritative source for self-guided learning – with more than 30 million copies sold worldwide – the *Teach Yourself* series includes over 300 titles in the fields of languages, crafts, hobbies, business and education.

British Library Cataloguing in Publication Data
A catalogue record for this title is available from The British Library.

Library of Congress Catalog Card Number: On file

First published in UK 2002 by Hodder Headline Plc., 338 Euston Road, London, NW1 3BH.

First published in US 2002 by Contemporary Books, A Division of The McGraw-Hill Companies, 4255 West Touhy Avenue, Lincolnwood (Chicago), Illinois 60712-1975 U.S.A.

Cover illustration by Mike Stones
Typeset by Transet Limited, Coventry, England.
Printed in Great Britain for Hodder & Stoughton Educational, a division of Hodder Headline Plc, 338 Euston Road, London NW1 3BH by Cox & Wyman Ltd, Reading, Berkshire.

Impression number   10 9 8 7 6 5 4 3 2 1
Year   2007 2006 2005 2004 2003 2002

Contents

Absolutism   1
America   2
Anarchism   3
Anti-Semitism   4
Apartheid   5
Aristocracy   6
Autarky   7
Bolshevism   8
Bourgeoisie   9
Capitalism   10
Christian Democracy   11
Civil Rights
    Movement, The   12
Class   13
Classics   14
Communism   15
Conservatism   16
Conspiracy Theory   17
Constitutional Monarchy   18
Corporatism   19
Cultural Memory   20
Darwinism   21
Decolonization and
    Post-colonialism   22
Democracy   23
Dictatorship   24

Emancipation   25
Enlightenment Thought   26
Environmentalism   27
Ethnic Cleanising   28
Eugenics   29
European Unity   30
Existentialism   31
Exploration and Discovery   32
Fascism   33
Federalism   34
Feminism   35
Feudalism   36
Folklore   37
Gaullism   38
Genetics   39
Genocide   40
Globalization   41
Guild System   42
Humanism   43
Ideology   44
Imperialism   45
Industrialization   46
Intellectuals   47
Isolationism   48
Jacobins   49
Kafkaesque   50

Keynsian Economics   51
Left, The   52
Leninism   53
Liberalism   54
McCarthyism   55
Machiavellian   56
Maoism   57
Marxism   58
Mass Politics   59
Medieval, The   60
Migration   61
Modernism   62
Monarchy   63
Multiculturalism   64
Myth   65
Nation-state   66
Nationalism   67
Nationalization   68
Nazism   69
Nihilism   70
Pacifism   71
Post-modernism   72
Proletariat   73
Propaganda   74
Psychoanalysis   75
Racism   76

Reformation Thought   77
Religion   78
The Renaissance   79
Republicanism   80
Revolution   81
Right and The
   New Right, The   82
Romanticism   83
Rule of Law   84
Science   85
Secularization   86
Separatism   87
Social Democracy   88
Socialism   89
Sovereignty   90
Stalinism   91
State, The   92
Syndicalism   93
Technocracy   94
Terrorism   95
Totalitarianism   96
Trade Unionism   97
Trotskyism   98
War   99
Welfare State   100
Zionism   101

Introduction

Welcome to the **Teach Yourself 101 Key Ideas** series. We hope that you will find both this book and others in the series to be useful, interesting and informative. The purpose of the series is to provide an introduction to a wide range of subjects, in a way that is entertaining and easy to absorb.

Each book contains 101 short accounts of key ideas or terms which are regarded as central to that subject. The accounts are presented in alphabetical order for ease of reference. All of the books in the series are written in order to be meaningful whether or not you have previous knowledge of the subject. They will be useful to you whether you are a general reader, are on a pre-university course, or have just started at university.

We have designed the series to be a combination of a text book and a dictionary. We felt that many text books are too long for easy reference, while the entries in dictionaries are often too short to provide sufficient detail. The **Teach Yourself 101 Key Ideas** series gives the best of both worlds! Here are books that you do not have to read cover to cover, or in any set order. Dip into them when you need to know the meaning of a term, and you will find a short, but comprehensive account which will be of real help with those essays and assignments. The terms are described in a straightforward way with a careful selection of academic words thrown in for good measure!

So if you need a quick and inexpensive introduction to a subject, **Teach Yourself 101 Key Ideas** is for you. And incidentally, if you have any suggestions about this book or the series, do let us know. It would be great to hear from you.

Best wishes with your studies!

Paul Oliver
Series Editor

Preface

This book offers 101 explorations of some of the ideas which have shaped British, European and World history. One of the pleasures of writing it has been selecting which material to include and how to present an instant introductory perspective. This has meant that much has had to be left out or glossed over. The interpretations which I offer are guided by a wish to reflect up-to-date scholarship and to excite renewed interest in the 'history of ideas' and the 'ideas which have shaped history'. This book is not a definitive guide but aims to support study and to spark further reflection.

Even a relatively slim volume is often the product of a surprisingly long list of individuals who have assisted in its publication. Helen Hart, Paul Oliver and the Hodder team have been very supportive throughout the different stages of the book. Thanks must also go to several other colleagues who have all assisted along the way: Keith Jenkins, Sue Morgan, Ken Lunn, Giles Scott-Smith, Jonathan Charteris-Black, Pilar Munoz-Juan and Barbara Rassi. My colleagues at University College Chichester, Jonathan Woolfson and Benjamin Noys, deserve special mention for their helpful comments on a draft of the book. All the remaining deficiencies are my own.

Absolutism

A bsolutism is the theory or practice of complete rule of the state by a monarch or dictator. In purely abstract terms, absolutism is a form of state organization.

Historians working in the nineteenth century first identified the period of broadly 1660–1789 as 'the Age of Absolutism' in Europe. This was a time when monarchs like the French 'Sun King' Louis XIV (1638–1715) governed with seemingly unlimited power. The Monarch was placed over and above other men and was perceived as selected by God. The authority of the state was centralized and the influence of provincial landowners and notables was withdrawn. In political theory, the King both made and was above the law. Feudal restrictions of religion, law and custom were ended. Great palaces like that of Versailles, Paris, symbolized the authority of the heads of the royal households.

The idea of absolutism has been subject to detailed historical research and theoretical reflection. For left-wing historians, often inspired by the writings of Karl Marx (1818–83) and Friedrich Engels (1820–95), the period of absolutism represents a state of 'late feudalism' in which the landowning class placed all authority in the King so as to limit peasant revolt. For other scholars, less influenced by Marx, the historical task has been to analyse the scale of absolutist power. For example, some 'revisionist' historians have suggested that the absolutist power of monarchs in the seventeenth and eighteenth centuries has been exaggerated. Kingly power even at its highest point was not without restriction. One might even argue that a pure state of absolutism had never been witnessed in Europe. Or, rather more elegantly, as one leading British historian put it, it is clear that 'certain monarchs were more absolute than others'. So, in comparative terms, one was more likely to find fully developed absolutism in Spain, Portugal and France than anywhere else in Europe.

see also...

Feudalism

America

America exists not only as a geographical space. It also stands for a particular political and social outlook. For example, in a broadly positive sense the phrase 'American Dream' describes the opportunities associated with living in a liberal, democratic and capitalist society, specifically the United States.

The idea of the American Dream was re-enforced by visions of the United States as a frontier society in which expansion and growth were not only phases of history but also more spiritual characteristics. To an extent, this view of the historical destiny of the United States grew out of the period of westward expansion in the nineteenth century. The Gold Rush and the development of the West Coast cities of California underpin it. It is also implicit in the historical reconstructions of the frontier period offered by USA's most famous of historians: Frederick Jackson Turner (1861–1932). Since Turner, numerous leading American politicians and others have developed this conception of the nation and 'its mission'.

The close association between the United States and capitalist economic organization has also often meant that critics of capitalism have used the notion of America in a very negative light. Here the term 'America' is almost always used to denounce capitalist economic life and the culture that goes alongside it. This was evident in communist critiques of America during the Cold War (1945–89). However, it is a less known fact that anti-Americanism was also common in many non-communist European intellectual movements as well. For example, in the 1930s French authors like Robert Aron spoke of the 'American cancer', while others on the far right-wing of the political spectrum saw America's multicultural cities, notably New York, as sinister examples of race mixing.

Whether or not the huge intellectual and symbolic investment in the idea of America has ever helped ordinary Americans go about their daily lives is disputable. The associations placed on the name of their country by friends or enemies are to an extent beyond the control of the inhabitants of the USA.

Anarchism

Anarchism is a social, economic and political doctrine that argues for the absence of government or leaders. Today's retrospective, popular, images of anarchism as the politics of chaos is somewhat misplaced. The stereotype of a bearded, bomb-throwing, man is more a product of the bourgeois imagination than of anarchism itself.

Anarchist thinking dates from the time of the French Revolution (1789) and grew in Europe in the nineteenth century. Key anarchist thinkers included Pierre Joseph Proudhon (1809–65), Michael Bakunin (1814–76) and Peter Kropotkin (1842–1921). Unlike many other ideologies, such as liberalism, communism or fascism, there has never been an anarchist society or example of anarchism 'in power' or as a fully functioning 'regime'. However, in the early part of the last century anarchism was especially strong amongst French, Italian and Spanish trade union movements.

A key principle of anarchism is opposition to the state, government and law. Authority, including the Church, is dismissed. Likewise, private property – capitalism – represents a third force of order which is to be challenged. Instead of the capitalist liberal democratic state, broadly, anarchists considered that individuals should be allowed complete freedom in society. Institutions that stand for order have to end for this to occur. Subsequently, the development of non-state, anti-hierarchical, federal, social-communal life would provide something like the ideal form of social organization. Very generally speaking, anarchism is a utopian doctrine which confronts and contests the state. Its own emphasis on liberty, and its diverse sub-strands of thinking, means that there has not been a single anarchist tradition but many, with regional and national differences. One important issue over which anarchists have frequently disagreed is method. Some anarchists look to quasi mystical spontaneous change, others to more organized revolutionary violence or terrorism.

Anti-Semitism

This is anti-Jewish belief or political activity, which in its complete form can be a coherent political ideology. While the Nazi policy of genocide took anti-Semitism to the most extreme of conclusions, anti-Jewish sentiment predated this organized form. From the late nineteenth century key European intellectuals, conservatives, socialists and others shared a variety of racial prejudices against the Jewish community. However, anti-Semitism was not born in the contemporary period. Predominantly, its origins lie in far earlier Christian thinking which held that the Jewish people were responsible for the death of Christ. From at least the late medieval period onwards successive waves of anti-Semitism marked European history. However, by the 1870s the religious grounds on which anti-Jewish hatred was based moved to a secular pseudo scientific racial prejudice.

In the inter-war period anti-Semitic groups or Nazi-style parties existed across Europe. Nazi and other anti-Semitic literature was cast in the form of popular conspiracies in which the Jews were accused of presenting a dangerous threat to Aryan populations. Nazi propaganda consistently used the Jew as a scapegoat to explain the military, social and economic miseries of post-World War I Germany. Ultimately Nazi anti-Semitism evolved from full-scale abuse of civil rights to the open street violence of the Crystal Night riots against Jewish property (9–10 November 1938). A politics of genocide (the Holocaust or 'Shoah') began in early 1942.

After the liberation of the Nazi death camps public dissemination of anti-Semitic views has been restricted to fringe groups of the far right-wing. By the 1990s the rise of the internet provided a new technological space where anti-Jewish spokespersons have flourished. Typical of recent anti-Semitism is the contention that the Holocaust had not taken place. This viewpoint is a new articulation of the old conspiracy theory writing.

see also...

Conspiracy Theory; Genocide; Nazism

Apartheid

Apartheid is an Afrikaans word meaning separation or 'apartness'. It was first used in South African political debate in the 1930s. Its common usage is to define the South African regime which was built on the basis of racial segregation from 1948 to 1990. For three decades a racially divided state survived and prospered. Resistance to apartheid by the African National Congress (ANC) and others, often in the face of extreme intimidation, ended the regime in the 1990s.

The policy of apartheid was formally ushered into South African politics by the electoral victory of the Afrikaaner National Party in 1948. In general terms the policy on race had been sketched out in the Party's 'Report on Race' in 1946. This document signalled that the National Government wished to assert the segregation of whites from non-whites. This was to be combined with a removal plan of Africans away from cities to designated rural zones. However, in a contradictory stance, the white farmers and industrialists were not to lose the important asset of cheap African labour.

Two of the key masters of apartheid were Prime Minister Malan (1874–1959) and Prime Minister Hendrik Verwoerd (1901–66). In their periods of governance many of the main legal structures which created the apartheid state were implemented. The Populations Registration Act (1950) defined all citizens according to their race. This was accompanied by acts prohibiting inter-racial marriage and sexual relations. In the same year the Group Areas Act stopped mixed communities and destroyed those African settlements which were located in White South Africa. Infamously, the Johannesburg suburb of Sophiatown was destroyed and grotesquely renamed 'Triumph'. Africans were to be settled in ten 'homelands' or 'bantus'. African freedom of movement was regulated and prohibited by an extensive pass system. In short, apartheid was a model of racism in governmental practice.

see also...

Racism

Aristocracy

Originally this term is derived from the Greek meaning 'rule by the best'. In the study of history it is most commonly used to describe the privileged social cast to have held power in Europe from about the early Middle Ages to the eighteenth century. This group is also sometimes described by other expressions including the terms nobles or nobility.

The aristocracy were those families who held economic power through the ownership of land. In turn, political power was conferred by the gift of special entitlements and privileges from the King. These entitlements were transferred across generations on the basis of the 'hereditary principle'. This meant that sons inherited the social-political privileges of their parents. Alongside the royal households these groups represented the European élite. They were protected by their own strength and the rules of the Feudal system. Similarly, the power of the Church and the belief that God had dictated each man's place within the social hierarchy kept the social world in order. This idea of 'divine right' justified the powerful position of the land-owning aristocrat over the toiling peasant farmer.

From the French Revolution (1789) onwards the aristocracy has declined. The idea of democracy leaves little room for hereditary privilege. Nevertheless, historians have shown that in terms of economic strength the nobility did not really disappear from view. Rather than being outmanoeuvred by the rising middle classes the landed aristocracy often became successful in the capitalist economy. Bourgeois respect for aristocratic culture also bolstered their symbolic position. In addition, democratization occurred far later in many European countries than the national histories of Britain or France suggest. For instance, Russia, Germany and Austria only democratized in the twentieth century after revolution (1917) or military defeat (1918). Moreover, even under the British constitutional monarchy the second chamber of the Houses of Parliament, the House of Lords, maintained some aristocratic influence on politics into the twentieth century.

Autarky

Autarky is a twentieth-century term which is used in the field of economics. It describes a government economic policy which prioritizes the domestic economy over international free trade. Vital national economic resources such as food, power, or heavy military industry are brought under the self-sufficient control of the state on the principle that they are too important to be left to be supported by more random external forces. Very few experiments in pure autarkic policy have ever formally taken place. Importantly, the term should not be confused with when a nation-state faces isolation because of international trade sanctions. Autarky refers to a *deliberate* system of economic self-sufficiency, not an imposed one. It is a *conscious* rejection of international trade and the liberal marketplace. A classic measure to encourage autarky is to levy high tariffs (charges) on any foreign imports so as to encourage the use of domestic goods.

Probably the most notorious attempt at autarkic economic management was that developed in Hitler's Third Reich (1933–45). Under the leadership of Dr Hjalmar Schact, the Nazi economy prioritized re-militarization, flagrantly ignoring the agreements of the Treaty of Versailles which had strictly limited German rearmament after World War I. However, Schact's measures were held to be insufficient by Hitler and he was dismissed from the post of Economics Minister in 1937. Other less well-known flirtations with a policy of autarky include aspects of British Imperial control and American isolationism. That all the major experiments in this form of economic management took place in the 1930s is not coincidental. The Wall Street Crash (1929) prompted the search for many different new ways of avoiding economic depression. However, in the postwar period autarky has passed from economic favour. In an age of economic globalization there is little to suggest that autarky will regain any popularity.

see also...

Globalization

7

Bolshevism

Bolshevism is a word derived from the Russian *bolshintsvo* which literally means 'majority'. This was the term selected by Lenin to name his faction within the Russian Social Democratic Labour Party. In contrast to the 'majority', Lenin named his opponents in the movement the 'minority' or the Mensheviks. After the revolution of 1917 the Bolsheviks triumphed and the Menshevik faction was suppressed. In 1918 the Bolsheviks revised their name to the All Russian Communist Party (Bolshevik). Further alterations of the name followed in 1925 and again in 1952. The Bolsheviks ultimately emerged as the Communist Party of the Soviet Union (CPSU).

The Social Democratic Labour Party was a Marxist inspired revolutionary movement which agitated against the Tsarist state both inside and outside of Russia. Divisions among the revolutionaries came to a head at their second Party Congress in July 1903. Significant differences developed between the various leading exiled Marxists over the nature of their political movement and the role that it should play in furnishing a revolution in Russia. For Lenin, as demonstrated in his essay *What is to be done?* (1902), the political party had to lead and to expect complete loyalty from its membership. Others in the movement, notably Martov, believed that membership required a wider social appeal. Further internal antagonism developed when the election of the board of the party newspaper, *Iskra*, was discussed. It was in this context that the Party was divided between pro-Lenin 'Bolsheviks' and pro-Martov 'Mensheviks'. In retrospect, the historical documents which chart the debate appear to suggest doctrinal hairsplitting. However, for Marxist revolutionaries, issues of the theory of revolution were important. Words mattered. Similarly, Lenin was seeking to establish power within the revolutionary movement.

see also...

Leninism; Marxism

Bourgeoisie

This French term is used to describe the middle class. Today it is usually employed by social and cultural historians to discuss those groups in eighteenth- and nineteenth-century European society which emerged as economically powerful under capitalism. It is in the light of the theory of history offered by Karl Marx (1818–83) that so much historical attention is devoted to the group.

Engineers, industrialists, bankers, successful tradesmen and shop owners can all be understood as the middle class. Similarly, the professions of lawyers, doctors, civil servants, university scholars and teachers are also frequently analysed for being part of the bourgeoisie. Classically, each of these very different groups forms the single class based on the fact that their social-economic success was won by individual effort instead of privilege. For Marxists, this marks the bourgeoisie as distinct from the aristocracy. However, revising Marx, it is open to interpretative debate what values or practices the different middle class groups really shared. For example, much divides a lawyer from an engineer and so on. Nevertheless, it remains credible to broadly talk about these people as a distinct group based on their shared economic success under capitalism.

It should be underlined that the emergence of the middle class varied enormously across Europe. It was more prominent in those parts of the continent in which industrialization and capitalist economic development had occurred, such as Victorian Britain or nineteenth-century France. Elsewhere where rural and quasi-feudal life maintained its importance, the class was less evident. This was especially the case in Russia, much of Central and Eastern Europe as well as the underdeveloped Mediterranean.

see also...

Class; Marxism

Capitalism

This is the dominant economic system that has marked the history of the West since at least the sixteenth century.

The central feature of the system is the exchange of goods or services for monetary value or, to put it crudely, 'cash'. However, capitalism does not rely solely on a one-way exchange between the producer of the goods, or the provider of the service, and the customer. Instead it is quite common, indeed essential, that groups exist and thrive in the space between the producer and buyer. These 'middle men' have the capital or cash to buy original products and then to sell the product on at a further profit. The middle men provide the service of distribution but in so doing gain riches from a product that they neither made nor need for their practical survival. This is the essence of the free trade marketplace. It is underpinned by the belief in the right to the private ownership of industrial production and the cash to buy products or invest in production.

A further 'middle man' group is necessary to the process. This group is made up of financiers who provide loaned cash for either producers, middle men traders or customers. Finance therefore also stands at the heart of the capitalist system. The freedom of money to stimulate either production, trade or consumption keeps the system alive and functioning. Without the supply of loaned money it seems likely that capitalism could not flourish. Capitalism developed alongside industrialization and this is a further key feature. Production under industrial circumstances is no longer based in the small workshop but because of the need to reduce costs so as to increase cash profits for the owner of the industry, there is a strong tendency within capitalism towards mass production. The use of huge factories and distribution chains allows for what is called 'economies of scale'. Or, to put it simply, mass production reduces the producer's costs.

These are all just some of the features of capitalism. They begin to indicate the complexity of the economic history of the modern and contemporary periods.

Christian Democracy

Christian Democracy is the name given to the leading West European conservative parties which were established after 1945. The title reflects their strong associations with the Church and some less direct affiliations with more traditional Catholic political parties of the inter-war period. In Italy, despite governmental instability, the Democriazia Cristiana (DC) held power throughout the Cold War period. In West Germany, the Christian Democratic Union (CDU) was similarly influential. The CDU Chancellors of Germany have included Konrad Adenauer (1876–1967), Ludwig Erhard (1897–1977) and more recently Helmut Kohl (b.1930). The French Christian Democratic movement was however significantly less successful. Although participating in coalition governments of the 1950s, the party was swept aside in the events which surrounded the fall of the French colony of Algeria. In 1958 the return of General Charles de Gaulle (1890-1970) to the French Presidency ended Christian Democracy in France.

Some general characteristics are definable across the different Christian Democrat parties. Each of the movements has drifted away from Catholic anxiety about the workings of capitalism to an enthusiasm for liberal economics. Turning its back on the fascist and Nazi past, the Christian Democratic right-wing is rigorously constitutional. Regarding foreign policy, both Italian and German Christian Democratic groups were sympathetic to the United States. What is more important, however, Christian Democratic politicians were central to the establishment of international unity in Europe. Reconciliation between Germany and France was critical to Chancellor Adenauer's foreign policy. The idea of a federal European state is also popular across Christian Democratic opinion. Importantly, the idea offered a springboard for post-Fascist reconstruction and a containment of European nationalism.

see also...

Conservatism; European Unity; Federalism

The Civil Rights Movement

This is the term given to those groups who campaigned for full African-American Rights in the United States, especially in the 1950s and 1960s. They included the National Association for the Advancement of the Coloured Peoples (NAACP) and the National Urban League. Perhaps the best-known scene from the movement is that of its figurehead, the Reverend Martin Luther King Jnr (1929–68), addressing the Washington DC Rally of August 1963. It was at this momentous gathering of approximately a quarter of a million protestors for black civil rights that King made his 'I have a dream' speech.

Although the American Civil War (1861–5) had been fought principally over the issue of slavery, reconstruction had not brought about equality for all Americans. Court rulings such as *Plessy v. Ferguson* (1896) had maintained inequality. Whites continued to be privileged and the black population in the South continued to be treated based on racism. The legal challenge for greater equality came in a second legal case, the famous *Brown v. Topeka* (1954). In this action black and white segregated schooling was challenged for being unconstitutional. Segregation was halted. However, southern white reaction was frequently violent. Infamously, federal military intervention was required to defend the co-racial schooling in Little Rock, Arkansas (1957). Ultimately several further major legal measures were used to respond to the Civil Rights Movements' continued efforts to establish equality. The 1964 Civil Rights Act was of great importance, as was the 1965 Voting Rights Act. For example, the later legislation resulted in a major extension of the black voting franchise. Democracy was being extended to all citizens of the United States.

By the mid-1960s the question of extending civil rights in social and economic legislation divided the movement. Likewise, the assassination of King in 1968 robbed it of a powerful leader. Previously peaceful protest was radicalized by the issue of war in Vietnam and the development of the wider 1960s counter culture.

Class

Class is the descriptive label used by historians and sociologists to define a group of people who share a common economic status. Generally speaking, historians of the modern and contemporary world analyse the interactions and characteristics of the three main classes: the upper class, the middle class (or the bourgeoisie) and the working class, sometimes also called the proletariat. Historians use the category of class to make generalizations about how social groups behave, how they respond to economic pressures or organize themselves into coherent political organizations.

Most studies of class draw on the original approaches to the subject which were developed separately in the nineteenth century by the two German thinkers Karl Marx (1818–83) and Max Weber (1864–1920). Karl Marx was the first to systematically discuss the notion of class. It plays a central role in his writings. In brief, the core of the Marxist definition of class is the economic status of the group in question. In nineteenth-century Europe Marx identified two major classes. On the one hand, there were those who controlled economic life and held property. They were the bourgeoisie. On the other hand, there were those people who did not possess property and had to work for a wage. They were called the proletarian class. Both these groups, or classes, are defined by their economic status. And, in Marx's wider political thought, they are shown to be drawn into constant conflict which will ultimately lead to a proletarian revolution against the bourgeoisie.

Significantly, Weber contended that social classes were determined by more than economics alone. Classes could also be identified based on their shared living conditions, experiences, access to power, education and the skills which they might offer to the marketplace. Classes were determined by a combination of economics and wider status.

see also...

Aristocracy; Bourgeoisie; Marxism; Proletariat

Classics

Classics is the study of the civilizations and cultures of Ancient Greece and Rome which existed some 2000 years ago and which have influenced political, artistic and philosophical life across the ages. At its heart is the aim to better understand that vital period of history and to analyse it. The methods of exploring this period include philosophical reflection on figures such as Socrates or Plato, as well as more practical archaeological investigation into the physical remains of Greek and Roman culture. The linguistic study of Greek and Latin and the translation of key texts into contemporary English is also a central issue in the field. Each new translation of a classical text provides a fresh way of reading its meaning. The reading and repeating of the Greek Myths are probably the most common engagement with the period.

In addition, according to a recent introduction to the field by the Cambridge-based scholars Mary Beard and John Henderson, contemporary classical study also emphasizes engagement with the tradition of *classical scholarship* itself. Therefore, reading classics also means focusing on the different periods of European history in which classical civilization was a central intellectual concern. For example, medieval scholarship looked back to Athens and Rome. Renaissance life was highly marked by an interest in the classical. In the modern period, the Victorians frequently made 'Grand Tour' visits to the sites of temples and monuments in the Ancient World. Typically the explorers from this period would bring all manner of objects and items back to London to be housed in museums and other grand repositories. Therefore, the classical scholar today is stimulated by the opportunity of exploring not only the Ancient world but each of these various historiographic restagings of it. The exploration and analysis of the classical tradition is as vibrant a source of scholarship as the more direct engagement with Ancient civilization itself.

Communism

Although a relatively common term in twentieth-century political history, the word communism has two distinct meanings. First, the word is taken from the philosophy of history developed by Karl Marx (1818–83) and Friedrich Engels (1820–95) in which it is used to describe a utopian future society. This case is outlined in the famous pamphlet *The Communist Manifesto* (1848). Marx and Engel's communist society represented the perfect condition of humanity in which there would be equality and no need for a state bureaucracy. Men and women would be able to live in social harmony. Here, the emphasis is on the idea of collective or communal organization in which all economic activity is led by the community instead of the individual.

Secondly, and more commonly, communism is also the word often used to describe the thinking of Marx and the various political movements and regimes which have adapted his doctrine. It is used interchangeably with the term Marxism. For example, 'communism' or 'communist' were frequently the terms that were used as the name of those political parties which were arguing the Marxist case. Thus, from 1918 the All Russian Communist Party (Bolshevik) governed Russia until its collapse in the 1990s. In France and Italy, significant communist party organizations developed in the inter-war period and were, by the late 1940s, two of the largest political movements in Western Europe. Beyond Europe, the most notable communist regime and party were those developed by Mao (1893–1976) in China. Fidel Castro's (b.1927) governance of Cuba is a further example of a communist state 'in practice'.

In the wake of the collapse of communist states in Europe, a high degree of historical re-evaluation has marked the study of communism. This is typified in Stéphane Courtois's *The Black Book of Communism* (1997).

see also...

Bolshevism; Leninism; Maoism; Marxism

Conservatism

Although some conservatives would deny it, claiming to be pragmatic rather than ideological, conservatism is a political ideology. Conservatives have always been interested in shaping the world around them. The core feature of conservatism is the protection of order and tradition. All change is rejected unless proven impossible to resist. Existing authority is to be defended. At the heart of this 'conserving process' are the institutions of the family, the rule of law, the Church and the organic, or Natural, national community. For conservatives, each of these notions have stood the test of time and are therefore preferable to unproven, potentially harmful reforms.

Regarding economic policy, conservatism has been divided. Two distinct subgroups are identifiable: the paternalist interventionists and the liberal free-marketeers. Paternalist conservatives believe that government has a role to play in successfully managing the national economy through mechanisms of intervention such as taxation or subsidy. Here, the conservative preference for social order and national success is predominant, with the stronger members of the community assisting its weaker elements. Conversely, overlapping with nineteenth-century liberalism, more free-market oriented conservatives emphasize free competition. Crudely, they advocate minimal, or zero, economic intervention, even if this might mean short-term suffering for some members of the national community.

Conservatism has been a highly successful force. Politically powerful, one historian has described the British twentieth century as the 'conservative century', underlining the ideology's consistent electoral success and its administrative predominance.

see also...

Liberalism; The Right and The New Right

Conspiracy Theory

onspiracy theories are interpretations of politics which emphasize the influence of secret and evil forces in the shaping of society. Typically, the tellers and believers of conspiracy theories argue that some small secret group of conspirators is responsible for everything of importance in the political arena. In the contemporary period these types of interpretation are alarmingly common. For example, they have been used to explain everything from the growth of the European Union to the assassination of the US President John F. Kennedy (1917–63). To the author's knowledge, no single conspiracy theory of this type has ever been demonstrated to be true. However, the idea of the conspiracy has proven a rich inspiration in contemporary literature, ranging from the American Thomas Pynchon's *The Crying of Lot 49* (1965) to Umberto Eco's world famous *Foucault's Pendulum* (1989).

However, it should be remembered that there is also a very sinister side to the political application of conspiracy theories and the psychological make-up which supports them. Notably, late-nineteenth-century and twentieth-century anti-Semitism was frequently based on the allegation that the Jews were a conspiratorial group. As the historian Norman Cohn explained, it was the typecasting of Jews as evil conspirators against Aryan Germany that culturally contributed to the Nazi policy of anti-Semitic genocide. Moreover, even after the Holocaust it is not uncommon for groups on the extreme right-wing to believe in re-worked versions of the old anti-Semitic conspiracy theory. This is also the case with many of the anti-United Nations, anti-World Government militia movements which have grown up in the United States in the 1990s. The world view of these groups is deeply rooted in conspiratorial assumptions and is coloured by a paranoiac belief in 'conspiracy'. The new technology of the internet provides a perfect site for the circulation and popularization of conspiracies.

see also...

Anti-Semitism

17

Constitutional Monarchy

This term describes states in which the rule of the monarch has become limited to ceremonial duties. Constitutional monarchies have existed across the world in various forms and at different times. For example, this was the constitutional order in France in the nineteenth century (1815–48). However, the best-known example of a successful constitutional monarchy is that of the British royal family. Here, the monarch is politically impartial. He or she has no right to rule or to intervene in politics. All political responsibility is held by the elected parliamentary executive and the legislative chamber. The nineteenth-century constitutional theorist, Bagehot (1826–77), is frequently quoted as having defined the unchanging nature of the British monarchy 'to be informed, to encourage, and to warn' but not to rule. The role of the royal house is a symbolic one. At home it represents a point of national unity which transcends class and regional boundaries. Externally, the monarchy reflects British identity across the world. The monarch is the head of state. The maintenance of the royal household suggests national strength through tradition and continuity.

Historically speaking, then, constitutional monarchies represent the route by which dynastic houses have survived in the face of the modern world and the democratization of government. In fact, very few royal houses managed to evolve into tenable constitutional monarchies. Comparatively, in the international context, British history is a rare example of democratization without a successful republican revolution. In the modern period, after the Civil War and brief Commonwealth interlude (1649–60), the British monarchy survived by conceding its position before anti-royalist activity became too strong. The reduction of the royal house to a symbolic role within the constitution limits criticism and leaves parliamentary democracy to fulfil the political, social and economic needs of the people.

see also...

Monarchy

Corporatism

This is an economic and political theory which explores the relationship between society, the state and the management of the economy.

Corporatists aim to create a system of state economic control which avoids the excesses of either liberal economic freedom or communist intervention. In the place of these two extremes, corporatist thinking invites employers and trade unions to negotiate with the state to resolve their tensions in the best interests of the nation. Corporatist thought therefore identifies key groups (different producers, workers' representatives and organizations, the state bureaucracy) and allows them to shape economic policy through collaboration. An underlying theme of this process is that each group is reliant on the other and that they have mutual obligations. Evidently, corporatism is influenced by social Catholic thinking and is anti-Marxist in its conception of the relations between the social classes. The idea of interest groups being defined on the basis of their economic function also echoes the medieval guild system.

Corporatism is a twentieth-century European idea which has attracted a variety of supporters. Most commonly it is associated with Fascism and Mussolini's attempts to form a corporatist state in Italy. However, in practice, Italian fascist corporatism was a failure and resulted in centralism. Despite its unhealthy associations with the extreme right-wing, corporatist thought remained relatively influential in the post-war period. In 1950s France, Charles de Gaulle's (1890-1970) first political party, the *Rassemblement du Peuple Français*, advocated corporatist partnerships. Several other West European economies were also influenced by corporatist ideas in the resolution of industrial conflict. Moreover, at a European level, the Treaties of Rome (1957) which formed the first structures of the European Union included elements of corporatist doctrine.

see also...

Guilds

Cultural Memory

In the 1990s, historians and others have been frequently concerned with issues of cultural or collective memory. They used these often interchangeable terms to define the processes by which the past is remembered in the present. The theoretical base on which the subject is founded lies in the work of the sociologist Maurice Halbwachs. His studies from the 1930s were the first major analytical pieces to question how societies, groups or individuals remember.

Special historical focus has been reserved for the ways in which periods of trauma and upheaval have marked twentieth-century Western society. For example, numerous historians have studied how Europe remembered the horrors of the First World War. Adopting innovative methods of cultural history, they have taken as their subjects war memorials, literature, history-writing, architecture, film and poetry. These sources provide evidence of how peoples came to terms with conflict, death and defeat.

Hinting towards theories of Freudian psychoanalysis, historians have also explored how nations have not fully faced their records of civic shame. For example, much work has explored the problem of German war guilt in the light of the Holocaust of the Jews. In France it is almost taken as axiomatic that the country for many years afterwards failed to confront its predominantly pro-Nazi era of collaboration. This Freudian 'repression' was only broken in the early 1970s by powerful novels and films which showed the extent to which the French had assisted in the German occupation. Perhaps the definitive example of this shift in cultural memory was the documentary directed by Marcel Ophüls, *The Sorrow and the Pity* (1970/71). More sensational fictional works which are perceived by historians of memory to have broken taboos about fascism included the film *Lacombe, Lucien* (1974).

see also...

Psychoanalysis

Darwinism

In 1859 Charles Robert Darwin (1809–82) published his theorization of the evolution of life on earth, *The Origin of the Species*. The term 'Darwinism' identifies his thought and the thinkers who have perpetuated it. Darwin's analysis of the development of species and their gradual changes over the history of the earth was a radical departure from Christian explanations of the creation of man and his environment. Instead of a providential creation, or a series of recreations (such as following the Biblical Flood), Darwin argued that species had changed on a long and gradual basis. Man had evolved as a descendant from animal predecessors.

From 1837, following a period of five years as a serving naturalist on *HMS Beagle*, Darwin was convinced that geological evidence suggested that the earth had changed over long periods of history. More radically, it seemed that nature too had adapted. It was plausible that only those species that had adapted to new geological factors had survived. Darwin contended that these new species had not been mystically created but had descended with some modification from their ancestors. Biological, and indeed human, history could therefore be mapped based on the continuity of basic features that were inherited and new characteristics which were produced over time and perhaps in response to conditions. To paraphrase further, species variation would occur over many generations based on natural selection. Natural selection crudely means the fortuitous selection of characteristics which guarantee one species' adaption and survival, or another's extinction.

The twentieth-century science of genetics has modified and supported the central claims which Darwin made about life on earth. Nonetheless, for huge numbers of people across the globe – believers of all the major world religions – Darwinian explanations of creation have had little impact.

see also...

Genetics; Science

Decolonization and Post-colonialism

From approximately 1945 onwards the European nation-states withdrew from their imperial territories. For some powers this process was a negotiated recognition of their limited strength following the Second World War, while for others bitter wars were fought before surrendering control of the Empire. Independence movements struggled for their freedom from colonial oppression and to establish their own nation-states. The word decolonization is used to describe the complex processes which marked these conflicts.

Probably the most violent experience of decolonization was witnessed by the French and their anti-imperial opponents. Wars of decolonization were fought and lost firstly in Indochina (1945–54) and then in Algeria (1954–62). War in North Africa brought about major constitutional reform in metropolitan France and subsequently provoked a domestic crisis which plausibly could be interpreted as a civil war. Only the strength of President de Gaulle's policy of gradual withdrawal and the suppression of pro-colonial terrorist groups in France led to a final resolution and redefinition of France's place in the world. In contrast, British decolonization was a far less violent affair. Independence was frequently negotiated and granted to formerly imperial subjects. For example, the Indian Independence Act (1947), passed by British parliament, created two new states: India and Pakistan.

Legal and practical decolonization occurred relatively quickly. It is evident that the psychological and cultural movement away from an imperial mind-set is a far more complex process. The complications of living after imperialism are often labelled by scholars as 'post-colonialism'.

see also...
Imperialism

22

Democracy

Today, democracy generally describes those systems of government in which all individuals have a right to play a political role and to be represented in government. Democracy is therefore associated with the holding of regular and free elections, a plurality of political parties, freedoms of speech and association, as well as the rule of law. These practices are commonly associated with liberalism in the phrase 'liberal democracy'. Democracy itself is not a political ideology but a concept concerning the way societies are governed.

Historically, the idea of 'government by the people' was of limited importance until the eighteenth-century Enlightenment. Subsequently, in both the American (1776) and French (1789) revolutions, the people began to claim the right to self-government. It was no longer acceptable for an individual or an élite group to manage the state without the participation of the mass. As Abraham Lincoln most famously expressed in his Gettysburg address: 'government of the people, by the people, and for the people' (1863). However, the installation of democratic government was neither instant nor straightforward. Only a series of revolutions firmly established the idea of democracy in nineteenth-century France (1830; 1848; 1870). In Britain, a gradual series of acts of parliament extended the notion of popular representation in government (for example, the Great Reform Act 1832). In Russia, Germany and the Austro-Hungarian Empire only defeat in the First World War (1918) prompted the end of dynastic absolutism. Moreover, even in the democratic states of Britain, France, Switzerland and Belgium, women were often not perceived to have political rights or to be worthy of political representation. This limitation was not redressed in many nations until the enfranchisement of women after 1945.

see also...

Emancipation; Enlightenment Thought; Republicanism; Revolution

Dictatorship

Dictatorship is a word which describes a particular form and style of government. The key characteristic of a dictatorship is that the state is controlled by a single individual or single political party. Generally speaking dictators are not members of the royal households but are commoners. The dictator, or wider dictatorial group, controls all aspects of the state and is not limited by a sense of legality. However, this does not mean that dictators do not make laws. Simply, it is that the laws that are promulgated under a dictatorship are based on the exclusive will of the dictatorial group. On this basis, the governance of fascist Italy, Nazi Germany and Stalinist Russia are frequently described by contemporary historians as 'the Dictatorships'. The period in which they were established is also often comparably labelled the 'age of the dictators'. The term is therefore frequently used very loosely to mean something very similar to the word 'Totalitarianism'. However, the origins of the word dictatorship do not necessarily point to all of its twentieth-century connotations. The term is far older and was in fact first used in the classical Roman Republic. In this context, it referred to the office held by an individual who was empowered during periods of extreme crisis.

Definitions of twentieth-century dictatorship have also often suggested that the society in which the dictatorship reigns is itself a victim of the dictator. In this usage 'dictatorship' is partially defined by a lack of popular consent from the populace. Instead of support, the power of the dictator is won by threat or more subtle coercion. The issue of 'lack of consent' is however problematic. While of course many groups and individuals resisted the Nazi or fascist dictators, it should also be noted that other groups in Germany or Italy were supportive.

see also...

Totalitarianism

24

Emancipation

This word means to free or to release from restriction. In historical interpretation it is strongly associated with the freeing of slaves from ownership. For example, the cessation of serfdom in Russia was pursued through Tsar Alexander II's 'Edict of Emancipation' (1861). The phrase 'the emancipation of women' is also frequently used but in a somewhat different context. It is employed by commentators to describe the history of the struggle for the political rights of women.

The idea of emancipation is a central part of the history of the abolition of slavery in the United States of America, before, during and after the Civil War (1861–5). For example, on 1 January 1863 President Abraham Lincoln (1809–65) asserted his Proclamation of Emancipation. This act effectively liberated slaves from ownership. The proclamation was underlined in Lincoln's Gettysburg address. Here, on the site of a bloody civil war battle, the basic constitutional principal of 'equality before the law' was reasserted by the President. The very destiny of the independence of the United States was linked to this belief. Lincoln began his speech with the words: 'our fathers brought forth on this continent, a new nation, conceived in Liberty, and dedicated to the proposition that all men are created equal.'

Full emancipation of the slaves was incorporated into the United State's constitution in its thirteenth amendment (1865). However, it should be remembered that these legal assertions of emancipation had been established only on the basis of military success and the violence of the civil war. They had also been underpinned by the work of *abolitionists* in America and elsewhere who had campaigned for the end of slavery. Southern slave masters had never wanted to reform their economic system but instead had sought succession from the United States to defend their position of power.

see also...

The Civil Rights Movement

Enlightenment Thought

The term Enlightenment describes the major philosophical and intellectual developments which occurred in Europe during the eighteenth century. This era is sometimes called the 'Age of Enlightenment'. Its key feature was man's questioning of previously securely held beliefs in the supremacy of God, the Church, the monarchy, and much else besides. The period gave rise to the usage of the French word *philosophes* to describe the era's thinkers who circulated their new knowledge in literature, music, philosophical tracts, encyclopaedia and other writings. Among the well-known thinkers of the period one can note John Locke (1632–1704), Voltaire (1694–1778), Denis Diderot (1713–84), Jean-Jacques Rousseau (1712–78), Carl Linneus (1707–78), Claude-Adrien Helvétius (1715–71), Montesquieu (1689–1755), David Hume (1711–76), Immanuel Kant (1724–1804) and in science, Sir Isaac Newton (1642–1727). In 1784, Kant defined the period's major contribution as having been an urge for the individual to 'use his intelligence without direction from another'. On a political level, much Enlightenment thinking contributed to the fall of the monarchy in France in 1789. Enlightenment thought, although sometimes challenged, has remained the baseline of the western world's intellectual development until the late twentieth century (and although some twentieth-century philosophers might disagree, potentially long into the future).

Today many of the ideas that we probably still hold as 'common sense' were established during the Enlightenment. These include our scepticism of God, the importance of democratic representation of the individual and a preference for the rational over the irrational or romantic. The *philosophes* believed in the power of human enquiry to generate a purely rational science of society.

see also...

The Renaissance

Environmentalism

nvironmentalism is the belief in, or study of, man's essential interaction with the natural world. Its roots lie in the field of geography and the word is sometimes used interchangeably with the term ecology. Since at least the 1960s, both environmentalism and ecology have been used without much rigour to describe the economic, social and even theological beliefs that emphasize the preservation of the natural world. In politics, the term 'Green' or Green Party has been adopted to suggest an equivalent position.

Environmentalists argue that both economic and political developments in modern times, from, for ease let us say 1789 onwards, have had a terrible impact on the natural world. To paraphrase, ideological groups like socialists, conservatives, liberals, fascists or communists, all wrongly placed man at the centre of their doctrines. They all neglected the fact that humans live in the natural world. These modern political movements sadly failed to recognize the need for politics to embrace mankind *and* its environmental context. To paraphrase the views of the Greens further, economic growth and industrialization has systematically led to a dangerous destruction of nature. The case is put by environmentalists that these combined processes have led to global ecological disaster. Political ambivalence and industrial expansion have threatened the balance which existed between mankind and the environment.

In the final decades of the twentieth century a variety of green solutions were posed in response to the concerns that have been briefly summarized. In France and Germany, Green political parties entered left-wing coalition governments. Numerous non-governmental pressure groups also influence states and wider public opinion, for example, Greenpeace.

see also...

Industrialization

27

Ethnic Cleansing

This expression came to prominence during the end of the twentieth century during the break-up of the state of Yugoslavia (1989–2000). It was used in this context to describe the military, political and cultural desire of an ethnic group to eliminate the presence of all other ethnic groups within its defined territorial state. For example, in the fragmentation of Serbia, Croatia, Bosnia and Kosovo it was common to hear areas of territory being described as having been 'ethnically cleansed'. This meant that they had been made mono-ethnic and were subsequently in the control of a single ethnic group. This was a violent and terrifying process. The forced movement of communities from one zone to another was accompanied by extensive murder, the rape of women, and the destruction of any signs of cultural or religious presence within the territory.

The politics of ethnic cleansing was shocking to Western observers of the Yugoslav crisis. On a limited scale it appeared that a politics of racial purification in direct comparison with the anti-Semitic policies of the Nazi Third Reich was reoccurring in Europe. However, one would have to make a number of qualifications to the emotive analogy, without wishing to diminish the horrifying nature of ethnic cleansing. Importantly, a politics of ethnic cleansing need not be genocidal. It is simply the forced removal of an ethnic group from its home to another place. Likewise, Yugoslav ethnic cleansing operated within the territorial boundaries of the former Yugoslavia and, unlike the Nazi persecution of the Jews, was not conducted on an international scale. On the other hand, the equation between genocide and ethnic cleansing should not be too quickly dismissed as false historical analogy. In a practical sense the two processes are very similar. Much of the redrawing of the Yugoslav ethnic map was based on violence and racially inspired murder. This was the case in a number of exemplary incidents, perhaps the most famous of which was the Serb massacre of Bosnian Muslim men in Srebernica in July 1995.

see also...

Genocide

Eugenics

This term was first used by the British scientist Francis Galton (1822–1911). It is used to describe the belief that mankind should be 'improved' on the basis of controlled breeding. The theory was popular in Britain, the United States and Europe for much of the inter-war period. However, it was horribly coloured by élitist and racist assumptions.

Eugenic planning can be of a number of different types. On the one hand, eugenic groups can argue that breeding should be politically encouraged between strong humans who display the genetic characteristics which the eugenic planner believes will improve society. On the other hand, other social groups who display genetic weaknesses can be prohibited from breeding. Much of this race science supported Nazi anti-Semitism. However, recent historical research has shown how widespread these views were among politicians and the intelligentsia in the liberal democracies. Galton was influential in the British universities. He worked closely with University College, London. Moreover, many in the wider artistic and opinion-forming community shared his ideas. The idea of creating human perfection was especially attractive to intellectuals who believed that they knew the key elements for such a future society. Less thought was given to the fate of those groups that did not 'fit' the eugenic plan.

Eugenic policy making did not become law in Great Britain. It was implicitly part of the Nazi statutes on race. For example, marriage between Aryan and non-Aryans was forbidden in Hitler's Third Reich. Likewise, the growth of the German Aryan family was supported by state awards for 'good' motherhood. Rather more surprisingly eugenic planning was also incorporated into some states within the USA. Sexual sterilization laws for some groups were introduced.

In the post-1945 period eugenics has been discredited. However, it has remained a historical shame for those who were associated with it.

European Unity

Across history a common 'European' homeland stretching from the Breton coast to the Ural mountains has been recognized. In different periods its geographical boundaries have changed. At times the idea of Europe has incorporated the British Isles and Russia, whilst at other points in history a more narrowly defined territory has been asserted. In the 1950s, politicians saw the possibility of European unity. In different ways Churchill, Monnet, Adenauer and others all argued for European collaboration or integration. From this lead the legal mechanisms and institutions of the European Union (EU) have come to represent Europe.

The thinking that lies behind the EU is derived from socialist and Christian Democratic federalism. At its core is the principle of the rule of law through multi-level federal government and liberal economic expansion. The post-war context of the enterprise is also important. After the shame of Nazi and fascist regimes, the Germans, the French, the Italians and others desired a major reorganization of governmental structures. This was an opportune moment to create reconciliation and unity. Europeans wanted to assert democratic understanding against nationalist hatred.

The EU version of European unity has evolved over time. Firstly, between 1952 and 1956 membership was limited to six nations working on the integration of their coal and steel industries (Belgium, France, Germany, Italy, Luxembourg and the Netherlands). These nations signed the Treaties of Rome in 1957 and thereby formed the Common Market. By the 1970s a widening of the European club followed to include Britain, Ireland, Denmark (1973), Greece (1981) and the Iberian powers of Spain and Portugal (1985). After the Cold War and the reunification of Germany, new expansions added the membership of Austria, Finland and Sweden (1995).

see also...

Christian Democracy; Federalism

Existentialism is a major philosophical interpretation of the human condition. It is especially associated with the philosophers Søren Kierkegaard (1813–55), Edmond Husserl (1859–1938) and Martin Heidegger (1889–1976). In twentieth-century France, Jean-Paul Sartre (1905–80) was the best-known representative of this school of thought. Sartre's perspectives were developed through numerous philosophical statements such as his book *Being and Nothingness* (1943). They were also explored through literature and drama. Sartre's play *In Camera* (1947) is perhaps the best-known theatrical exploration of existential thought. This is the source of the famous statement 'Hell is other people'.

Existentialists offer an explanation of human consciousness and the turmoils that this state brings to us all. To paraphrase further, human consciousness is based on no preordained external power (for example, God). The implication of knowing that our existence is rooted in this state of 'nothingness' is terrifying. However, it also brings

many othe...
that the way...
based on our ...
actions and thei...
According to exist...
people are unable to...
enormity of a life base...
'nothing'. Instead of con...
reflecting on and re-creati...
identities, they are seduced...
leading 'inauthentic' lives in w...
ideas of limited importance act...
vital crutches. Likewise, knowing...
that we are only ourselves, we loo...
for empowerment through
interactions with other people.
However, the individual's
consciousness determines the
status of these interactions.
Existentialists must choose how to
handle their own identities. In this
process, mankind can achieve
freedom. However, the idea of
existential freedom does not offer
an unproblematic life. In this
philosophical world-view, freedom
means mankind's right to struggle
with his own condition. It means
the right to think about his own
consciousness.

ration and Discovery

The fifteenth and sixteenth centuries witnessed European expansion across world. At the beginning of the rly modern period, Europe's nowledge of the rest of the globe was limited to North Africa and the wider Mediterranean basin. By 1600 the Americas, much of Western and Eastern Africa, as well as India and parts of the Far East had been discovered. Explorers and adventurers, predominantly from Portugal and Spain, but quickly followed by British and Dutch, had changed the idea of geographical space forever. This process is often described by historians as one of 'exploration and discovery' or the 'age of discovery'.

In 1488 Portuguese explorer, Dias, rounded the Cape of Good Hope for the first time. Just 12 years later his countryman Cabral located Brazil. On the Spanish side, Christopher Columbus discovered America in 1492. Spanish conquests of Southern America and the famous destruction of the Aztec civilization followed with the Cortès' expedition to Central America in 1519. Notoriously, the importation of European diseases, notably smallpox, eliminated many Aztecs. The motives that sparked European expansion are diverse and refute simple generalizations. They include economic, political and religious issues. For example, Catholicism and the idea of 're-conquest' supported Spanish endeavours. For the Portuguese, trade and the opening of shipping routes to lucrative spice markets were a central motive for discovery. Portugal's maritime merchant class saw exploration as a critical aspect of their commercial interests. The attraction of finding new sources of gold was another important stimulus. Commercial rivalry between the two dominant Iberian powers also encouraged the missions of discovery. Alongside economics, technological innovation in the maritime field underpinned the entire process, for without scientific revolutions in navigation and shipbuilding, European explorers would have been unable to so successfully embark on their voyages.

Fascism

istorians use the term 'fascist' to label groups, movements and regimes that share extreme right-wing values and policies. Generally speaking, they are referring to those movements which came to power in the 1920s and 1930s in Italy and Germany. The word fascist is derived from the Latin word *fasces*. Originally, this expression was used to describe a symbol which represented authority in Ancient Rome. In 1919, Benito Mussolini named his political movement the *Fascio di Combattimento*.

Fascist doctrine is centred on a belief in the greatness of the nation, the need for leadership and authority in government and the sublimation of the individual to the greater needs of the fascist party and the patriotic community that it represents. As well as these broadly totalitarian attitudes towards government and society, fascism is reliant on several highly negative stances. For instance, consistently it is anti-liberal, anti-egalitarian (and thus élitist), anti-capitalist and anti-communist. Fascism is also likely to be racist and anti-Semitic as with

the best-known fascist organization, the German Nazi Party. Fascist economics are usually corporatist. In addition, as argued by Roger Griffin, fascism has been identified as being highly reliant on myths and symbols of rebirth. Fascists are frequently concerned with destroying a decadent 'sick' old order to replace it with a 'healthy' 'New Order'. There is much evidence to support this perspective. Italian fascist and Nazi groups employed propaganda which was coloured in this way. The doctrine thrives on binary divisions of the world. For example, the struggle between good and evil, the patriot and the traitor, or in its racial mode, the Aryan and the Jew.

Since 1945 the term has been used as a political insult. In particular, communists tried to discredit their opponents by identifying them as fascist. Today only the most radical members of the extreme right-wing continue to declare themselves fascist.

see also...
Anti-Semitism; Nazism; Racism; Totalitarianism

Federalism

Politicians, political philosophers and intellectuals frequently explore how best to organize contemporary government. The most common twentieth-century means of managing the state in Europe has been the centralized nation-state. However, federalists have offered a very different perspective on these issues. In direct opposition to the idea of a single national administration, federalists argue that the most efficient and appropriate form of governance is multi-levelled. Drawing on traditional Catholic notions of the individual's relationship with God, federalists consider that a series of tiers of government should be empowered and work with each other. Thus, firstly, man is linked to his family setting; secondly, there is the local or regional community; thirdly, there is the level of national government and subsequently the continental or international arena. Federalists contend that good government is based on the sharing of power, responsibilities and duties across these levels. The notion of *subsidiarity* is critical to federalism.

Subsidiarity is the principle that dictates that political decisions should be taken at the level nearest to the individual or at that point within the federal structure that is best able to resolve the given political question.

Many different political ideologies have supported federal forms of government, including anarchists, socialists, anti-state liberals and others. However, in the post-1945 period federalism has been most popularly associated with European integration. For instance, a good example is the right-leaning Christian Democratic Movement which was powerful in West Germany and Italy. Christian Democrats and others have argued that a European level of government should be founded as the top tier of a continent-wide federal structure. Much of the thinking and practical application of federalism has therefore supported the creation of the European Union.

see also...

Christian Democracy; European Unity

Feminism

Feminism is the body of thought that combats sexual inequality and argues for the rights of women. Its origins date from the late eighteenth century when women first called for equal suffrage and participation in the liberal democratic electoral process. One of the earliest classic feminist works is Mary Wollstonecraft's *The Vindication of the Rights of Women* (1792).

After the battle for political and legal equality, a further wave of political and intellectual movements reactivated the cause of women's rights in the 1960s. At this turning point, the perspective of feminism went beyond the call for a restricted set of political rights to explore the role of women in society as a whole. Original social analyses, written by feminists, identified how patriarchy had dominated male-female relations across history. Western man – through power relations which are sometimes associated with the capitalist economic system – had used women's biological ability to bear children to construct inequalities. These inequalities always served *his* purposes. For example, the social-political roles of 'mother' or 'wife' controlled and structured women's lives. This system of control limited the freedom of women and it undermined equality.

Ending patriarchy poses several fundamental questions in feminist thought. Some feminists argue for a reformist approach to redress inequality by persuading men to reconsider their attitudes. This perspective implies that rationally when men realize they have oppressed women they will stop. Minimally, civic structures that affirm greater equality will be created. Here, the underlying principle is that men and women are 'people' who have much in common. Many different responses to patriarchy have also been detailed. For example, some feminists argue that the best response to male oppression is to celebrate how different women are from men. Women should create powerful cultural and social weapons through which to defend their sex and contest male domination.

Feudalism

Feudalism describes the dominant social, economic and political system in Western Europe which lasted from approximately the ninth to the fifteenth century and in parts of Eastern Europe to the eighteenth century. The system was based on a clear hierarchical social structure and the intricate management of property rights. At the pinnacle of the feudal world was the monarch. The monarch relied on the support of a number of leading nobles who, in exchange for the possession of land, provided the royal household with military support and loyalty. In turn, the nobility sublet lands to lesser nobles in exchange for farming or rent. At the bottom of the feudal system, peasants worked the land for their masters.

Two core characteristics of the feudal system should be underlined. Firstly, the system survived based on the acceptance that the social hierarchy was permanent and justified by God. This concept is sometimes described as the idea of 'Natural Order'. Secondly, in the feudal system the power of the Monarchy (to raise armies and to maintain support) was based on co-operation with the nobility. Thus, feudal Kings were not absolute. In an age of chaotic warfare, the monarch was dependent on his noblemen's ability to raise armies and to wage wars.

A number of complex factors brought feudalism to a close. In the field of politics and philosophy, the idea of the absolute monarch developed in the élite intellectual circles of the sixteenth century. Moreover, in the critical area of military activity, warfare became more organized and less dependent on the Lords. Likewise, feudal land ownership fragmented and richer peasants began to sell their produce to each other. Gradually the economic system of capitalism began to impose itself.

see also...

Absolutism; Capitalism

Folklore

G enerally speaking, folklore describes a society's longstanding culture and traditions. It is especially associated with those aspects of culture which date from the pre-modern period and which were not committed to paper, organized into formal museums or scientific categories. Instead, folklore is kept alive by song, popular storytelling and other legends which are passed down from one generation to the next.

The concept of naming these socio-cultural items 'folkloric' occurred in the modern period of European history. The expression was used for the first time by W.J. Thomas in 1846 and for much of the rest of the nineteenth century there was a popular scholarly rush to explore folk-poetry, folk-dance, folk-language and all other ancient national traditions. Perhaps the most famous thesis on magic, myth and legend is the study by the Glasgow-born J.G. Frazer (1854–1941). His *The Golden Bough* (1890) represented an attempt to systematically compare world legends and to explore their place in history. As well as academic reflection many societies and organizations sought to preserve traditions in the face of modernity. However, it is evident that many of these efforts to translate ancient or exotic culture into a contemporary setting were flawed. The original folklore could not be accurately replicated in the modern setting.

Historians today would no doubt see the rise of folkloric study as a clear signal for the passing of genuine folk custom. On the face of it, it would appear that the formal search for folkloric activity was the signal of the end of the more natural folklore traditions. However, while this argument looks attractive, it would be wrong to think that oral traditions or other popular beliefs ended in the nineteenth century. Many communities across the world continue to place great importance on customs that have never been formally controlled or put to paper.

Gaullism

Gaullism is the political movement in France inspired by the actions, policies and writings of General Charles de Gaulle (1890–1970). Both the leader and the movement have been critical in shaping twentieth-century French history. De Gaulle, a non-political military leader, first came to prominence during the Nazi defeat of France in 1940. On 18 June 1940 de Gaulle decided to continue fighting in the war and established his resistance movement in exile in London. Unlike any other French military or political leader, de Gaulle was not prepared to enter into any kind of collaboration with the Nazis. He therefore abandoned France and the official French army which remained loyal to the head of the Vichy regime, Marshal Philippe Pétain (1856–1951).

After the Allied victory, de Gaulle was welcomed as the liberator of his country. He had maintained French national pride and given vital leadership in dark days. However, while de Gaulle briefly served as President of the new Republic, by January 1946 various factors led to his resignation from office and the subsequent creation of a Gaullist political movement to channel his opinions. The first Gaullist 'Rally for the French People' party was founded in 1947. Its central values continued the spirit of the resistance. The movement highlighted unity, national pride, French independence and social corporatism. However, de Gaulle failed to regain office immediately and it was not until the crises of the French wars of decolonization that he returned to the Presidency. His second period of Presidential office came in 1958. It lasted until his resignation in 1969. In the interim period he had reformed the Republic into its fifth incarnation as a presidential system and presided over a decade of economic growth and European reconciliation.

De Gaulle's legacy is of central importance to French history, politics and culture. The political movement which he inspired continues to be active and is currently lead by President Jacques Chirac (b.1932). De Gaulle's own reputation is very high with broad support for his historical role coming from all sides of French political life.

Genetics

This is the scientific study of biological inheritance and the composition of life. This highly sophisticated field of research offers the twenty-first century much promise. Knowledge of genes and genetic activity across generations potentially anticipates the improved treatment of inherited illness. It may contribute to the reduction of disease and suffering experienced by man since his origins. However, the scientist's power to identify genetically transferred illnesses will also present society with new ethical choices about our power over life and death.

The historical origins of genetics are to be found in the nineteenth century and the studies of inheritance in peas conducted by Gregor Mendel (1822–84). His founding work – the essay 'Experiments in Plant Hybridization' – was published by the *Transactions of the Bünn Natural History Society* in 1866. Mendel established that life communicates hidden instructions that are not always externally visible. Codes or genes transfer important biological information across generations. However, some genetic features were dominant and visible while others were recessive or hidden.

The science of genetics was advanced in the twentieth century by numerous scholars. Its initial impetus was to an extent sparked by the desire to improve and perfect mankind (the idea of eugenics). This politically dubious project has been associated with work of Francis Galton (1822–1911). More valid research was conducted by the Dutch scientist, Hugo de Vries and in the United States by Thomas Hunt Morgan (1866–1945). Morgan's experiments on inheritance in the fruit fly were of great importance. He established that genes were integral to chromosomes and that different genes appeared to transfer different characteristics (e.g. wing length, eye colour). For the untrained layman the history of genetic research appears as a continuous story of unfolding complexity.

see also...

Eugenics

Genocide

This is the systematic policy of the eradication of a race and the traces of its historical and cultural presence. The word is most commonly employed by historians to describe the Nazi 'Final Solution'. This was the planned extermination of the Jews.

Nazi policy established a unique system of human cruelty that contributed to the deaths of approximately six million European Jews between 1941 and 1945. Thus, from the Nazi invasion of Russia in the summer of 1941, driven by an ideology of anti-Semitism, soldiers and special police groups massacred Jewish communities in central and eastern Europe. Scientific innovations in this task included the development of mobile units with 'gas-wagons' which could murder more efficiently than mere soldiers with guns. In January 1942 the Nazi Wannsee Conference instituted a more formal and systematic policy of anti-Jewish genocide. A total of six extermination camps, none of which was based on German soil, were developed. The names of these sites merit repetition:

Auschwitz, Belzec, Kulmhof, Majdanek, Sobibor and Treblinka. In these horrific places industrial methods of extermination were widely deployed to commit mass murder. For example, at Auschwitz, under the command of Rudolf Höss, Zyklon-B gas was first used for extermination in gas chambers. Approximately 1.5 million people suffered and died in Auschwitz.

Less well-known genocides than the Nazi attacks on European Jewry have also been witnessed. For example, at the end of the nineteenth and the beginning of the twentieth centuries, the little known Turkish massacres of the Armenians marked south-eastern Europe. More widely applied, and with a certain polemical edge, the term genocide is also sometimes used by writers to describe the White European settlement of North and South America and the consequent treatment of indigenous peoples.

see also...

Anti-Semitism; Ethnic Cleansing; Nazism; Racism

Globalization

Globalization emerged as a well-known concept in the late 1980s and more widely in the 1990s to describe the contemporary state of the world economy. The idea that the world was now a single marketplace, or globalized, was popularized in business management literature as the major trend in economics. For example, it was in this context that the Japanese guru Kenichi Ohmae used the aphorism 'Act globally but think locally'.

The economic theorists of globalization claim that life in the late twentieth century has taken on a global aspect. Commerce, stock markets and multinational companies make trade international. The development of satellite and computer communications and intercontinental flight has literally led to a shrinking of the planet. Perhaps the central characteristic of these forces of globalization is that nation-state governments are too small to offer much assistance to their citizens. National economic sovereignty has been lost. In its place huge multinational corporations, operating on a far larger scale than governments, shape the economic environment. These are the core features of globalization.

Among the commentators that agree that globalization has taken place there are fundamental disagreements about its merits. Defenders of globalization tend to be liberal economists. They note that the increase in free trade across the world can only benefit those who take part. However, the radical left-wing, especially after the fall of the Soviet Union, has taken up the cry of anti-globalization. They identify the forces of global capitalism with widening social injustice and the ever constant growth of US world power. In Western Europe the sub-terms '*Disneyfication*' or '*coca-colonization*' colourfully suggest the unwelcome cultural reach of American-led corporate power.

see also...

Sovereignty

Guild System

A guild is the name used for any specialist interest group or organization. Historically speaking, the guild system refers to the organizations of craftsmen, churchmen, scholars, merchants and others in the medieval and early modern period in Europe. Early banking or lending guilds were especially important in the area of finance. In education, guilds were established between teachers and students and thereby formed the basis of universities. In medieval Siena, Italy, the merchant guild was so powerful as to almost exclusively control the economic life of that city-state. In neighbouring Florence the 'lending' guild effectively controlled the currency of that city and established the florin as the most stable money in the region.

Generally speaking, guilds were established in towns and cities on the basis of crafts and other occupations. They offered the group protection and organization. For example, the guild provided a mechanism for the control of an entire trade within the city. The guild members were able to control the prices of their products or specialist labour. They established criteria for acceptable levels of quality of craftsmanship within their given field of activity. Guilds also provided education by establishing apprenticeships for the young to master their chosen trade. Politically speaking the guilds were also a powerful influence on the politics of city life. They acted in rather similar ways to our contemporary lobby or interest groups, seeking always to enhance the power of the sectorial group.

The rise of free trade and capitalist competition from the sixteenth century onwards marked the gradual decline of the guild system as a social and economic force in Europe. However, by the late nineteenth and early twentieth centuries some romantic nationalist thinkers looked back on 'the guild' with much nostalgia. In Britain this was especially the case in the writings of G.K. Chesteron (1874–1936) and Hilaire Belloc (1870–1953). Corporatist economic planning also draws extensively on the guild system.

Humanism

The term is derived from the Latin *humanitas* meaning 'pertaining to man'. It is generally applied to describe any philosophy or doctrine which takes as its central focus mankind. This concern is often placed in contrast to other interests, such as God. Historically speaking, humanism is associated with the Italian Renaissance of the late fourteenth and fifteenth centuries. However, it was also central to later enlightenment thought.

Central to Renaissance humanist thinking was a return to classical influences. Humanists believed that renaissance society could be improved if the correct classical ideas were followed and learnt. It was man's and society's duty to strive for greater achievements, drawn out from the examination of antiquity. Many humanists explored their ideas through the power of their own artistic creations. Art both allowed man to show off his technical ability as well as to demonstrate – through content – the importance of classical thinking. Raphael's magnificent painting 'The School of Athens' (1509–11) is one typical example. Similarly, the establishment of humanist educational institutions in, for example, Mantua and Ferrara, allowed the movement to expand. Key aspects of a humanist education were the areas of grammar, rhetoric, poetry, history and moral philosophy. The new development of the printing press meant that edition after edition of classical texts could be produced and disseminated. Sometimes identified by historians as one of the most influential figures of Italian humanism, the printer Aldus Manutius (1449–1514) established the Aldine Press in Venice for just this purpose.

Renaissance humanism both influenced reformation Protestantism and later the Enlightenment philosophers.

see also...

Classics; Enlightenment Thought

43

Ideology

Ideology or political ideology are two interchangeable words which are commonly used by historians to describe all political doctrines and their adherents. So, many of the terms that are explored in this book are ideologies. For example, socialism, liberalism, conservatism and fascism are all political ideologies. Each doctrine represents modern man's desire to understand, to respond to, and to shape the world. Exponents of 'ideological positions' demonstrate marked economic, political, social and cultural preferences. These propensities are not natural or innate but form part of traditions or families which are perpetuated by writers, thinkers, politicians, journalists and others. It is through the activities of these figures that political doctrines are moulded, sustained and reconfigured.

This brief definition of ideology is usually known as the truth-neutral approach since it avoids making value-based judgements as to what is or is not ideological. In Great Britain, it is associated with the work of the political scientist, Martin Seliger. However, very different, less open, usages of the term have also been employed. The originator of the word, Destutt de Tracy, used it to describe the science of ideas (1797). In the nineteenth century Karl Marx returned to the word but defined it very differently. In his writings ideology is used to account for the falsehoods and deceptions that mask society from seeing capitalist exploitation. Ideology, in the service of the bourgeoisie, conceals the workers from their own terrible plight. On the other hand, the Marxist philosophy of history is taken to be 'scientific' and true.

During the Cold War, American political theorists (for example, Daniel Bell b.1919) contributed to the confusion which often surrounds this most controversial of political terms by suggesting that after the fall of fascism and the decline of Communist Russia, ideology had in fact ended. To paraphrase, soon the liberal American model of pragmatism would triumph. As Marx before them, the liberal thinkers were defining ideology in a pejorative sense.

Imperialism

From the 1870s onwards European nation-states expanded greatly beyond their continent. Driven by rapid industrialization, they conquered much of the extra-European world by violence, trade and other forms of control. Resources such as gold, silver, diamonds, ivory, ebony, copra, cocoa, oil, coffee and cotton were exploited. This process was supported by major economic interests, governments of different political persuasion and constitutional organization, learned geographical and scientific societies, military leaders and the Catholic and Protestant Churches. In addition to economic motivation, a central spur to expand was the rise in European nationalism, supported by racist beliefs in natural superiority.

As the expression 'the scramble for Africa' implies, this continent proved one especially attractive territory to dominate in the late nineteenth century. While British, French, Belgians, Germans and others competed with each other in Africa, their expansion was also to an extent based on agreement.

Thus, the rules of intra-European expansion in Africa were signed at the Congress of Berlin in 1884. Nonetheless, national rivalry existed and brought Europe close to war on several occasions before 1914. In the imperial territories, barbarity and suffering were commonplace for indigenous populations. The word 'imperialism' is commonly used to describe this period of aggressive world conquest by the Europeans.

More conceptual definitions of imperialism are also employed by intellectuals and other experts. This alternative usage defines any central power's domination of culturally and/or ethnically different peoples within a loosely conceived geographical territory. This territory constitutes the Empire. Hence, one speaks of the Austro-Hungarian Empire, the Ottoman Empire or the Russian Empire.

see also...

Decolonization and Post-colonialism

Industrialization

From 1815 to 1914 Europe witnessed a period of significant industrialization. In the beginning of this period the vast majority of European economic activity was related to agriculture. However, by the final decades of the nineteenth century, in many parts of Europe this feature of life was replaced by a far greater proportion of mechanized, industrial, production. Of course, significant agricultural and small scale 'workshop'-based production continued. But, advanced technological processes of manufacture had increased to a scale far greater than that which had been experienced in the eighteenth century. This process is called 'industrialization'.

Patterns of industrialization varied significantly from nation-state to nation-state. Indisputably British industrialization had occurred first. It was also the most extensive in Europe. For example, the cotton mill sector led the way in the development of the factory as the new place of work; so much so that by 1870 historians have suggested that 50 per cent of the British working population was employed in these mass industrial centres of labour. No other European society shared this rate of industrial and social change. After Britain, Germany was probably the next most industrially active nation. However, it witnessed far later growth which was as sudden as it was dramatic. In the very brief time from the 1880s to the eve of the First World War, the German industrial workforce nearly doubled in number. Chemical and electrical firms became world-leading technologies. For example, the Siemens Brothers built the first electric power station (albeit in Britain not in Germany) in 1881. Elsewhere, in France and Italy industrialization was rather less widespread. Huge tracts of both nations remained highly agricultural. Nevertheless, they too witnessed regional industrial transformations which were just as important for their localities as the German and British cases.

Intellectuals

As with so many historical-political concepts, this word has many very different definitions. Generally speaking, intellectuals are people of learning and culture. Frequently, they are also prominent personalities who have dared to speak out on issues of popular concern. They are individuals who are not afraid to make decisions about the world around them and to then seek to alter it. Intellectuals are people who, based on knowledge and commitment, engage with political issues. Intellectuals frequently provide the clear thinking behind the political activism associated with all of the modern political ideologies.

The historical usage of 'intellectual' originates in Russia and France. In the late nineteenth century those groups in Russian society that were university educated and who felt dissatisfied with life under Tsarism were labelled 'intellectuals'. In France the term came into popular usage at the time of the Dreyfus Affair (1898). It was generally associated with novelists, journalists and others who publicly argued that the French establishment had wrongly accused the Jewish Captain Alfred Dreyfus of having betrayed his country. Emile Zola (1840–1902), the author of numerous novels, is most closely associated with this event. His pamphlet 'I accuse' first brought into public question the veracity of the French army's case against Dreyfus. Zola's artistic background and political interventions marked him out as a classic 'intellectual'.

Since the end of the Dreyfus Affair the term intellectual has been associated with France. It was especially used to describe the philosophers and artists who dominated cultural life from their café hideouts in Paris in the 1930s and 1950s. For example, the existential philosophers Jean-Paul Sartre (1905–80) and Albert Camus (1913–60) represented French cultural grandeur around the world.

see also...

Existentialism

47

Isolationism

solationism is a term that is used in the discussion of international relations. It describes foreign policies which favour the national self-interest by a withdrawal from international interventions or any other tightly constricting commitments.

Beyond its more general usage, isolationism commonly describes the foreign policy of the United States from independence to her intervention in the First World War in April 1917 and then the further retreat from European affairs which followed during the inter-war period. Isolationists are those groups in American politics who support this policy and argue in its favour. American isolationism was first advanced by President James Monroe (1758–1831) in 1819. His position asserted that only the United States has the right to engage in foreign affairs within the Americas. However, likewise, the United States would not 'interfere in the internal concerns of any of its [Europe's] powers.' The USA would not engage in the squabbles or even more ethical battles which might rage between the European powers. The moat of the Atlantic Ocean would always protect her citizens from the international anarchy of the Old World. For much of the nineteenth century the doctrine held, based not only on maritime geography but also on the dominance of the British Navy who would not seek conflict with the US.

To an extent, American involvement in the wars of the twentieth century made a mockery of US isolationism and swept aside its founding statement – the so-called Monroe Doctrine. The rise of hostility between the United States and Soviet Russia in the 1940s signalled its end. President Truman's 1947 statement that 'it must be the policy of the US to support free peoples who are resisting attempted subjugation by armed minorities or by outside pressures' announced to the world that the US would engage in a global foreign policy to protect states from Soviet intervention or communist subversion. This was the complete opposite of the Monroe position.

Jacobins

This is the name of a key political club from the period of the French Revolution. It supported the revolution of 1789 and by the early 1790s was especially associated with the radical revolutionary stance advocated by Maximilien Robespierre (1758–94). With Robespierre's own decline the organization ended in November 1794. At its high point of influence the Jacobins had been effectively part of the revolutionary administration of France.

Originally the term 'Jacobins' was derived from the Jacobins' convent where the club first met on the *rue St Honoré*, in Paris, in January 1789. Prior to this date the group had been called the 'Breton Club'. It was also sometimes labelled the 'Society of the Friends of the Constitution'. Beyond Paris, many other Jacobins clubs were established in the provinces of France. By the autumn of 1791 they numbered 83. One contemporary witness of the group's actions described it as 'the great investigator which terrifies aristocrats; [...] the great investigator which redresses all abuses and comes to the aid of all citizens,' (1791). Indeed, the Jacobins revolutionaries did appear to be closer to the people than many of the other organizations, newspapers and movements to emerge at that time.

The violence of the Jacobins' republican beliefs is well illustrated in the debates which raged over the future of King Louis XVI. The Jacobins, Robespierre and Saint-Just saw no philosophical or intellectual reason for the King to stand trial. In the opinion of Robespierre the monarchy simply had to be destroyed. This cold logic, and much of the 'terror' which followed, no doubt contributed to the association of Jacobins with the calculating and ruthless pursuit of revolution. Indeed, the term Jacobinism has become synonymous with the ruthless pursuit of revolutionary change which is driven by an élite leadership rather than the mass.

see also...

Bolshevism; Leninism; Revolution

Kafkaesque

This adjective is derived from the world described in the novels of the writer Franz Kafka (1883–1924). His posthumously published classic pieces, *The Trial* (1925) and *The Castle* (1926), illustrate many dark aspects of modern life. The narrator, known in both novels only as 'K', struggles to come to terms with the meaning and purpose of his existence. Moreover, sinister yet powerful bureaucratic structures seem to control his every move. Remarkably Kafka's fictional bureaucracies anticipate the alienation experienced by modern man in the capitalist system. They also predicted mankind's powerlessness in the face of either Nazi or Soviet totalitarian governments. The term 'Kafkaesque' evokes all of these anxieties. It is synonymous to living in a waking nightmare.

Briefly, Kafka's life provides some insights into his writings and outlook. Holding a doctorate in law, he worked as an administrator for an insurance company. However, his office life was viewed as a terrible block on his creative ambitions which were pursued outside of work. Family and sexual liaisons proved complex and unforgiving. However, in an irony which perhaps even goes beyond Kafka's own tormented imagination, his last request that his writings be destroyed was ignored. Thus, disobediently, Kafka's friend Max Brod oversaw the publication of the major novels in the 1920s.

Kafka's writings were translated and became popular and influential in the English-speaking world after the Second World War. To an extent they represent an oblique memory of that time. The echoes of the bureaucratic machinery which underpinned the Nazi Holocaust of the Jews are all the more poignantly underlined by the fact that Kafka was himself of central European Jewish origin, coming from Prague. In addition, his narratives of absurd alienation chimed with the post-war trend towards existentialism.

see also...

Existentialism

Keynsian Economics

This phrase describes the contribution of the modern liberal John Maynard Keynes (1883–1946) to the field of economics. His works, including *The General Theory of Employment* (1936), rejected the classic liberal belief that free market economies will regulate themselves and establish their own internal balance. In the period of depression which followed the Wall Street Crash (1929), Keynes suggested that the free market alone would not provide the solution to unemployment. Instead, he argued that government economic management and intervention could be used to invigorate economic growth. Two mechanisms were available. State spending on national projects (i.e. the building of schools or roads) would provide employment and turn previously unemployed workers into customers for other products. Alternatively, tax levels might be reduced to again make people more confident to spend money and thus generate economic activity. In addition, Keynes argued that governments should not always continue to balance their budgets but instead to create deficits to assist managing the economy.

In practice Keynsian economic theory at first proved controversial. In Britain, Ramsay MacDonald's Labour government was divided over how far to apply Keynsianism to combat the social cost of the depression. The issue led to the resignation of the maverick politician Sir Oswald Mosley who, after leaving the Labour Party, founded first the Keynsian 'New Party' and subsequently the British Union of Fascists. In the United States, President Roosevelt's 'New Deal' echoed much of the thinking of Keynes but did not fully support his analysis. Notably, the US government did not wish to run at a deficit. Nonetheless, the militarization of Europe and the outbreak of war in 1939 did however mean that national governments followed state intervention in the field of armaments, thus regenerating their economies via state spending. This was a state of affairs that continued throughout much of the Cold War.

The Left

The political label 'left-wing' originates in the period of the French Revolution. The phrase was first used to signify those who sat on the left-hand side of the King in the Estates General (1789). This grouping was composed of the 'Third Estate'; the group which was composed of people who were neither nobles nor clerics. Over time the layout of the Estates General has come to represent the classic spatial division in European politics. So, today, the expression 'the left' is frequently used as a catch-all term to describe all political ideas, parties and movements that are radical, reforming or revolutionary.

Among the many political ideologies explored in this book one can note: anarchism, socialism, social-democracy, Maoism and Marxism for being 'on the left' of the spectrum. Among these very different formations it is difficult to establish a definitive checklist of 'left-wing' characteristics. However, one can underline a general desire in all these groupings to work for social change. Most left-wingers show a willingness to believe that the basic conditions of life can and need to be improved. There is a sense of reforming zeal. Sometimes this is manifest through a sharing of Christian beliefs in equality and justice. Alternatively the ambition for change is welded to the secular theories of a leading philosopher or activist. However, many differences of opinion between different left-wing groups cannot be hidden. One of the classic divisions is between those who seek to work within the existing state (its governments and laws) and those left-wing groups that prefer revolution.

Spatial definitions in politics and history are not always as straightforward as they may seem. They are based on comparative and relational analyses which are likely to be subject to change. For example, ideas which were once considered 'radical' and therefore on 'the left' are likely to become accepted and even part of the conservative establishment.

see also...

The Right and The New Right

Leninism

Vladimir Ilyich Lenin (1870–1924) was the leader of the Marxist-inspired revolution in Russia in October 1917. The Soviet regime which was built around his interpretation of the work of Karl Marx maintained its independence for over 70 years, until a shift to liberalism in the 1990s. In that time it achieved mass industrialization of a predominantly rural society and a military victory against German invasion in the Second World War. Throughout its existence it challenged the assumptions of Western liberalism and the capitalist free market. 'Leninism' describes the Russian political leader's interpretation and subsequent application of Marxist ideology.

Leninism emphasized the need to create revolutionary change rather than to await the inevitable 'progression of history' via the economic development from feudalism to capitalism and subsequently to communism originally predicted by Marx. To this end, Lenin established the importance of the political party as the spark for revolutionary change.

It was the party and its leaders who would shape the revolution and prompt the working class to realize their revolutionary role. In this context, the mass of the peasants could also form a revolutionary group in the struggle against Tsarism and the putative forces of Russian liberalism. Writing on imperialism, Lenin identified the European nation-state's global expansion as a further factor in capitalism's downfall. International competition would lead to war and ultimately revolution. These views, expounded during the First World War, reflected that era and sought to explain it through a reworking of Marx.

After the Russian revolution and the civil war, Lenin fell ill and suffered a series of debilitating strokes. His thinking from this critical period is therefore incomplete. However, it is evident that the seeds of Stalin's later dictatorship were present in Lenin's early illiberal control of political opposition.

see also...

Bolshevism; Marxism; Stalinism

53

Liberalism

iberalism has proven to be arguably the most successful political ideology to mark Europe and North America in the nineteenth and twentieth centuries. Key liberal thinkers of its early periods have included John Locke (1632–1704), Adam Smith (1723–90), John Stuart Mill (1806–73) and Thomas Jefferson (1743–1826). In the twentieth century one thinks of the contributions of Margaret Thatcher among many others.

Liberalism's core belief is the freedom of man. They believe no force, including the monarchies of the feudal or absolutist periods, should restrict the rights of the individual. However, liberals believe that only the state and the rule of law can maintain freedom. Unlike anarchists, for liberals a society without legal structures and government bodies would decline into violence. The representative state, democratically elected, fulfills the function of providing order so that liberty of opportunity can flourish equally. However, in case the ruling state itself becomes too strong, liberals prefer government via the balance of power because this divides and weakens the state into the executive, the legislature and the judiciary.

Liberalism advocates a free market, or capitalist, approach towards the economy. Liberals consider that a key freedom is the right to property. In addition, man might accumulate more wealth through his labours and ingenuity. For liberals no force should impinge on man's right to gain wealth by legal means. Again, the rule of law, specifically 'the contract' is important. If a commercial agreement meets the legal authority then it should be unhampered by the state.

see also...

Conservatism; Keynsian Economics; The Rule of Law

McCarthyism

McCarthyism dates from the Cold War period of American history. The word is derived from the name of the anticommunist Senator Joseph McCarthy (1908–57). McCarthy broke onto the national political scene when in 1950 he denounced the Truman presidency for harbouring communists and communist sympathisers in its administration. Notably, in a speech delivered in Wheeling, West Virginia, McCarthy asserted that 57 communists and 205 communist supporters were working in the State Department (the American Foreign Office).

This viewpoint was stimulated by a number of setbacks for the United States in the early period of confrontation with Soviet Russia. For example, the secrets of the atomic bomb, which had been exclusively held by the USA, had fallen into Russian hands. In the Far East, the right-wing Chiang Kai-Check had lost China to the Communist leader Mao Tse Tung. Instead of acknowledging the strengths of their enemies, or even just the ebb and flow of international affairs, Americans like McCarthy preferred to see conspiracies gnawing at the heart of their country. The phrase McCarthyism is associated with this type of unfounded anticommunist accusation. For some commentators the period was comparable to the Salem Witch Trials of earlier American history. Famously, this outlook was brought to the stage by the playwright Arthur Miller in his piece *The Crucible* (1953).

McCarthy continued his assault on the perceived procommunist 'establishment' into the 1950s. In 1953, he chaired an official Senate investigation against internal subversion. However, after the right-wing Republican victory in the 1953 Presidential elections, much of his case was marginalized. Reckless verbal assaults on figures with no hint of communism led to McCarthy discrediting his own position. The Senate passed a motion of censure against him in 1954. McCarthy's brief but dramatic period of fame was over.

Machiavellian

Current usage of the word Machiavellian describes politicians who use all possible methods to maintain and extend their power. This sense is derived exclusively from Nicolò Machiavelli's short political self-help book, *The Prince* (1513). This infamous text was written to advise rulers how to keep their power and privileges. It was drawn extensively from Machiavelli's own diplomatic career and the political culture of Florence where he served. Its inspirations were classical and contemporary, including the life of Cesare Borgia whose ruthless strategies Machiavelli admired.

Written as a series of instructions *The Prince* was a revolutionary study of political judgement and leadership. The book's most contentious claim was that the Prince did not need to lead a Christian life to govern with authority. In fact, for Machiavelli, the traditional notion of virtue might lead the Prince into error. Instead of piety, leadership required altogether different 'virtues' to those advocated by the Church. *The Prince* outlines these new strategies. For example, violence and ruthlessness were important weapons which should be used to serve the interests of the Prince. For leaders, it is preferable to be feared than to be loved. However, even the plans of the most adept ruler might fall victim to ill fate. On this point Machievelli famously suggested that the best countermeasure to Fortune was to be prepared for sudden change. A Prince who was able to adapt his position to the circumstances around him would always be most likely to succeed.

It is all too easy to see why Machievelli's book continues to be cited as a bible of modern politics. Its many admirers have included extreme right-wingers and the communist left. The British political adviser to Prime Minister Thatcher, Lord McAlpine, even went so far as to write a reworking of the original, *The Servant: A New Machiavelli* (1990). Nevertheless, it is somewhat harsh to read Machiavelli only as the father of cynicism in modern politics. His many other writings explored a greater range of issues than that of crude power.

Maoism

Maoism is the term used to describe the political doctrine of Mao Tse Tung (1893–1976). It represents a unique adaptation of Marxism-Leninism to twentieth-century China.

Mao refined Marxist-Leninist orthodoxy in a number of ways. Rather like Lenin before him, Mao justified a communist revolution in a fundamentally peasant society, which had yet to experience a genuine bourgeois revolution, or to develop a dynamic proletariat. Mao argued that the case of China was different from Western Europe and so need not follow classic Marxist lines of historical interpretation. The Chinese peasantry were a potentially revolutionary group because of their experience of feudalism and imperialism. Ultimately the size of the peasantry also meant their support was required for any successful revolution.

Mao also showed how the tactics of guerilla warfare could be used to overthrow oppression. His communist army would integrate itself within the peasant community for which it fought by treating them with respect. In addition, the abstract 'intellectual' nature of Marxism-Leninism was denounced in favour of more practical party interactions with the peasants, in which the masses were consulted directly as to their future. For example, this was tested in the Communist run Yan'an area.

After the chaos of the Second World War, on 1 October 1949, Mao declared the People's Republic of China. First, Mao followed Soviet 'Stalinist' models of industrialization. However, an alternative was sought. This was a rejection of forced industrialization in favour of the peasant commune. This 'Great Leap Forward' was abandoned by 1962 for more orthodox economic planning. Between 1965 and 1968, further innovation was announced: the Cultural Revolution. Identifying the growth of party bureaucracy and inefficiency Mao led the young to criticize all the faults in the system that they could identify.

see also...

Leninism; Marxism

Marxism

This term describes the writings and theories of the nineteenth-century German political philosopher Karl Marx (1818–83) and those political groups that have broadly accepted his work. Marxism is a systematic, intellectually stimulating, form of socialist ideology. It is an anti-capitalist, anti-liberal, economic explanation of the cause, effect and future of capitalism. Perhaps its defining feature is the importance ascribed to revolution. Reflecting on the economic and social upheaval of industrialization, Marx offered an account of world history which showed how exploited groups would one day revolt against the free market and bring about a more socially equitable world.

Marxist thinking is based on economic determinism (the inevitable impact of economic forces on mankind) and is derived from a philosophy of history which emphasizes social progress through class conflict. To paraphrase, society's modes of economic production determine how man lives and interacts with his fellow man in social classes. Revolutionary changes take place when economic crises provoke class conflicts. For Marxists this was the case when the French Revolution (1789) marked the end of feudalism. In a predictive sense, this would also be the case in the future when the working class overturns the capitalist middle class. Capitalists, in their drive to increase wealth, would exploit their proletarian employees in the factories to such an extent that the economic system would collapse. A utopian, communist state would develop. Here, private property would be abolished and the proletariat would control the state until it withered away. This course of historical progression, from feudalism to capitalism to communism, is the central strand of the Marxist philosophy of history.

Marxism's impact was enormous. It has influenced history and politics across the globe.

see also...

Bolshevism; Leninism; Maoism; Revolution; Socialism

Mass Politics

This phrase characterizes twentieth-century Western European and North American political life. It describes the broad period from the late nineteenth century to the midpoint of the twentieth century when governments first derived their support from all adults. The widening of the electoral franchise meant that political parties and their leaders had to conduct politics in a different style from the early periods. Now they had to engage with society as a whole, rather than only with its élites. In addition to mass enfranchisement, critical to this development were popular education, widening literacy rates and military service. The rise of the daily press was of equal importance because it provided a means of constant communication about politics for all types of readerships. Each of these forces socialized men and women towards an interest in national politics.

In the early part of the twentieth century those new ideologies which emerged during the birth of mass politics were especially successful at communicating with the new electorates. Fascism and communism both excelled at creating mass political organizations and produced propaganda that attracted wide approval. In particular, both these ideologies were able to apply new technology to communicate with national and international audiences. In addition to the press, the radio and the cinema were especially attractive tools. One might argue that totalitarianism was a classic response to the potential of mass participation in politics, society and economics.

By the end of the twentieth century electoral participation and mass political commitment were seemingly in decline in the liberal West. Approximately 60 years after political activists had first had to win genuinely wide support to gain power, it seems that a combination of apathy and cynicism have started to reverse developments.

see also...

Democracy

The Medieval

This phrase is the label used by historians to describe the duration of time in European history which broadly falls between the collapse of the Roman Empire and the emergence of the early modern period. While no single set of dates can be used to account for the period one might profitably locate the medieval era as being between, at the earliest, the fourth century and, at the latest, the end of the fifteenth century. The synonym 'Middle Ages' is also used to describe the same period. Moreover, the adjectives 'low' and 'high' add some further precision.

The Medieval period can be characterized by its social and economic structure. Broadly speaking, the practice of feudalism was the dominant form of social organization. Equally characteristic of the age was the rise and development of Christianity. For example, by 300 the Bishop of Rome started to be described as 'Pope'. Furthermore, across the entire period, the power of the institutionalized Church grew extensively. The religious concept of Christendom represented a central feature of medieval life. It was a defining marker of identity, being arguably akin to nationality or citizenship in the modern world. And so, gradually, pre-Christian pagan conceptions of religious practice in Europe were eroded or superficially surpassed by Christianity and the organized Catholic Church.

Aside from feudalism and Christendom, warfare and violence also marked society. Religious wars against invading pagans from the Scandinavian north, or Muslims from the south and east, were commonplace. The Muslim presence in Europe, north of the Pyrenees, was ended by Charles Martel's victory in the battle of Tours in 732, for instance. Crusades outside of Europe in the East culminated in the attack on Jerusalem and its brief capture in 1099. However, despite further waves of crusades in 1147 and on a third occasion in 1191, the Holy Land was never controlled by the Medieval West.

see also...

Feudalism

Migration

Human history has been a story of movement and resettlement. Frequently, peoples, languages and cultures have intermingled and mixed, as one group has encountered another. The word migration describes the processes associated with these exchanges. Firstly, it refers to immigration. This word describes the case when a group of people joins another culture. Secondly, it also describes the word 'emigration' meaning when people leave their homelands in search of new horizons.

Numerous examples exist of both forms of migration. For example, perhaps the Pilgrim Father's journey from Plymouth, Great Britain, to North America is the best-known example of emigration. And, again America's openness to immigration in the nineteenth and early twentieth centuries have made that country synonymous with immigrant groups. The very national identity of the United States is synonymous with openness to all.

Despite the historical propensity for migration, 'twentieth-century man',

with his emphasis on mono-cultural, mono-racial nation-states, has come to see immigration as a highly negative occurrence. This has been especially the case for Western Europe since the economic crises of the 1970s. Nations which had once sought migrant labour to fill their industries no longer felt able to accommodate groups of further newcomers. In response, nationalist and racist political groups, sometimes neo-fascist in style, have advocated a politics of anti-immigration. On more than one occasion, politicians of the conservative centre-right have shared these views. Notably, the end of the twentieth century witnessed a further migration crisis in Europe. The fall of the Soviet Union and the terrible break-up of Yugoslavia prompted significant population movements from eastern Europe to the West. To the south, political instability and poverty have also motivated Africans to attempt to settle in Europe. Europe's response has often been far from welcoming.

Modernism

Modernism is the retrospective label which scholars give to the predominant literary and artistic movement of Europe and North America between approximately the late nineteenth century and the 1940s. Examples of modernist literature include James Joyce's *Ulysses* (1922), Louis Ferdinand Céline's *Journey to the End of the Night* (1932) and William Faulkner's *The Sound and the Fury* (1929). In poetry no survey of modernism can ignore the contributions of Ezra Pound (1885–1972) or T.S. Eliot (1888–1965).

It is impossible to date the birth of modernism precisely. However, by the 1890s there was a marked shift in cultural sensibility which appeared to be responding to that age. This was captured in the criticism and fiction of the American novelist Henry James (1843–1910) and poet T.S. Eliot, for example. Their writings marked an end of the Victorian realist mode. In its place James captured the inner psychological subtleties of the characters that he chose to follow. Unsurprisingly, later modernism was influenced by Freud's theory of psychoanalysis. Modernists –

reflecting in many ways the social and emotional chaos of the First World War period – also experimented with form. Unpunctuated, free-flowing writing, drawn from diverse sources, including the classical and the popular, were used to etch out the interior thoughts of characters. Modernist writing was self-consciously difficult. It made little concession to the popular reader and it drew attention to itself as an art form. For some critics this élitism is questionable.

Beyond the world of literature, historians also use the term 'modern'. Generally speaking, they use it to describe the long period which followed the Middle Ages: the sixteenth, seventeenth, eighteenth and nineteenth centuries. The additional expression 'contemporary' is used to account for more recent historical developments, including for example, the period in which the artistic current of modernism first appeared.

see also...

Post-modernism; Psychoanalysis

Monarchy

This is the belief in the right of government of a single leader rather than an elected group of politicians. It is commonly associated with the belief in divine right and the special status that endows to the royal household. This means that the ruler of the society is decided exclusively by birth. The issues of qualifications or abilities are of no importance. This aspect of monarchy is also sometimes called the hereditary principle.

Historically speaking, two variations of monarchy have been common in Europe. Absolutist monarchs ruled over much of the modern period (the sixteenth to the nineteenth century). Theoretically, their power was total and represented a force for the centralization of the state. Among the many exemplary figures one can cite Louis XIV of France, or the entire Romanov dynasty which ruled in Russia until its overthrow in the revolution of 1917. On the other hand, more limited 'constitutional' forms of monarchy have also been common. The current British constitution in which the Queen has a predominantly ritualistic role is one typical example. This is the system of the so called 'constitutional monarchy'.

Monarchism is the political force which supports the idea of monarchy. It has been common in both societies in which a royal house has been in government and equally important as a counter-revolutionary force in the face of republicanism. Monarchism has also been faced with internal divisions over the issue of the choice of successors. For example, this was the case after the French Revolution (1789) when different groups of monarchists favoured different potential successors from the different lines of descent within the royal house. The issue was made even more complex by disputes over whether any future monarchy should perpetuate the absolutist tradition or instead to govern as a figurehead in a constitutional monarchy.

see also...

Absolutism; Constitutional Monarchy

Multiculturalism

In the late twentieth century the term multiculturalism is frequently used by journalists to mean anti-racism. In this context it loosely describes the maintenance of good cross-cultural relations in western European societies where different ethnic groups have come to live together following immigration. In Britain, France and Germany this has been especially the case from the 1970s onwards.

However, more academic, sociological, definitions of multiculturalism show how complex an issue is at stake. The more detailed perspective goes far beyond the idea of anti-racism. It defines multiculturalism as a model society in which different peoples are equal before the law but also free to maintain their preferred social and cultural traditions. In a genuinely multicultural society, citizens from whatever background would have equal educational opportunities and life chances without having to adapt their lifestyles to the dominant culture. For example, one could imagine an Indian, living in Britain, reaching the peak of his or her chosen profession while also maintaining a private life which was essentially Indian in its cultural choices. The right to be different is supported without the risk of losing legal or economic power.

In reality multiculturalism has not always been successfully achieved. It appears to be closer to being an aspiration than a description of the actual state of affairs. Numerous factors work against the achievement of multiculturalism. Indigenous groups do not like to see different cultures 'taking root' in their nations. These groups feel threatened and unsure of how to respond to the new presence. Likewise, many immigrants seek to abandon their distinct cultural identities in favour of the new dominant culture. Assimilation seems easier than potential conflict. Moreover, the dominant indigenous culture cannot be simply ignored and sidestepped. New hybrid cultures emerge.

see also...

Migration; Racism

Myth

Commonly, the word myth describes dramatic stories which on closer inspection are shown to be false. Recently, myths have also been analysed by historians, anthropologists and other social scientists. These scholarly observers have noted that very basic recurring types of story play a critical role in ancient and modern society. For example, across world history peoples have been fascinated with narratives of unity, conspiracy, revolution, national foundation or heroic saviours.

These myths, or sacred narratives, serve a number of political and social functions. They unite. They provide feelings of communal security and bring people with otherwise different social backgrounds together. In this use of the term, the status as to whether they are true or false is of little importance. The group that holds the myth will always perceive it to be true. Conversely, opposing groups will contest the myth and try to debunk it.

Mythic stories about politics, society, the past and the future do not appear from out of a vacuum. They are the products of individuals and groups who believe in them and seek to persuade others to believe. Artists, politicians, political activists, intellectuals, journalists and historians are the typical producers of myth in the secular twentieth century. Writing with a political purpose, these individuals live their lives telling accounts about the world which are coloured by their given ideological position. Mythic stories about politics, told from a doctrinal perspective, are the meat and drink of all ideologies. There are communist myths, fascist myths and so on. Political activists need stories to tell about the world to maintain their own beliefs and to persuade others to support them

It is helpful to conclude by asking what is not a myth? Briefly, any story that has little political relevance, is not a matter of doctrinal passion, or does not invite commitment, cannot be mythic. Any communication that is not told through a narrative, or is not reliant on the evocation of a narrative, is not a myth.

Nation-state

This word describes societies where the national community is congruent with its system of government. Nationalists have historically argued for the creation of this form of social organization and defend it against threats.

Although the nation-state might appear to be a very normal condition because today we live in a world of nation-states, their formation has been complex. It is easy to forget that other forms of governance and notions of community functioned before the birth of the nation-state. Man has not always defined himself on national grounds but formally created his identity on the basis of kinship, religion, trading groups, or his relationship towards the royal household.

The period of 1800 to 1950 is strongly associated with the rise of the European nation-states. For example, it is in this era that many of the major European nation-states were created. Belgium gained self-governance in 1830, Italy and Germany were united into single political regimes in 1870. It might also be argued that the formation of the French Third Republic (1871) concluded the creation of the French nation-state. After 1918, the collapse of the Austro-Hungarian Empire precipitated the creation of Czechoslovakia, Rumania, Hungary and Yugoslavia. While these new political entities were less ethnically diverse than the former Empire, they remained vulnerable to ethnic division. The 1990s break-up of Yugoslavia suggests that one is continuing to observe the formation of ethnically and culturally coherent nation-states in the Balkans.

Finally, the British nation-state is intriguing. Formed from the sixteenth century onwards it is based, crudely, on the English cultural group's dominance over its Celtic neighbours. It is easy to anticipate the complete secession of these groups from Great Britain. Ironically, this would come 150 years after the highpoint of nationalism in a time coloured by multiculturalism, globalization and internationalism.

see also...

Nationalism; Separatism; Sovereignty

Nationalism

This is the belief that the national community is the best location for government. As a single expression of political thought alongside liberalism it is arguably the most important concept to have shaped European history in the last 200 years. Since 1789 Europe has been marked by nationalists, the formation of nation-states and their rivalry in the two World Wars of the twentieth century. A vast range of different forms of nationalism has developed, including conservative, liberal and fascist versions. Two general conceptual comments help to introduce this key idea:

(1) Normally, nationalists believe in the unique organic qualities of their national community. Thus, nationalists identify a wide range of markers that they feel contribute to the creation of their national identity. These markers have included language, geography, culture, race, folklore, history or religion. For example, it is well known that the English are an island people, they are traditionally protestant Christians, and they hold a sense of history that underlines

their national strength in trade and warfare and naval supremacy. In particular, a history of democratic progress through parliamentary reform has instilled a conservative, anti-revolutionary, pragmatism in English political culture. For nationalists these markers of the community are not perceived as 'constructed' or false but are accepted as essential characteristics of the nation. They are the normal, every day, features of English identity.

(2) Once a national community has been imagined, the central nationalist expectation is that the community will achieve self-government. Very general historical patterns have emerged. On the one hand, nation-states have been formed by élite groups working from the centre outward. However, nation-states have also been directly formed by the community from below.

see also...

Nation-state; Separatism; Sovereignty

Nationalization

This is the economic policy of placing industry, services or resources under the ownership of the state. Commonly, it is associated with the reformist strategies of twentieth-century social democratic parties and their governments. Generally speaking, in the period following the Second World War much of Western Europe took industry under governmental control. This was a period when nationalization seemed highly favourable because it offered some social comfort to workers who might otherwise have looked to a Marxist-Leninist inspired revolution.

The British Labour Government programme of nationalization is a classic example of the strategy in the post-war era. It was conducted by an enthusiastically social democratic Labour Party whose constitution had promised the control of the 'means of production' by the people. Moreover, its leaders had planned in the wartime coalition government to build a more equitable society after the conflict. As the expression of the day ran, 'the heights of industry were to be stormed'.

The legislative programme of nationalization in the late 1940s was impressive. In 1946 the Bank of England, Coal Mining and Civil Aviation were taken into state control. The following year the railways were nationalized. In 1948, through 1949, the Gas, Iron and Steel Industries were added to the list. Ultimately about 20 per cent of British industry had been taken into the hands of the state. However, despite the impressive list, historians have noted the chaotic manner in which British nationalization took place. As one historian underlined: 'No plan or strategy seemed to exist.' Despite the obvious need for state planning in association with state-run industry there was little on offer from the outset. Similarly, it was unclear as to whether the new national industries were to serve a social purpose or to operate at a profit. This dilemma was never fully resolved.

see also...
Social Democracy

Nazism

The words Nazi and Nazism are derived from the name of the German fascist political party, the National Socialist Workers Party or NSDAP. It is uniquely associated with the political career of its leader, Adolf Hitler (1889–1945), and the party's governance of Germany between 1933 and 1945.

The NSDAP evolved from the early German Workers Party (DAP), which had been founded in Munich, Germany, in 1919 by Anton Drexler. In February 1920 the Party changed its name to the better-known title and produced its first coherent programme. This was nationalist and frequently denounced the Treaty of Versailles which had punished Germany severely for its perceived guilt in causing war in 1914. The NSDAP was also anti-Semitic and racist. Unlike in Mussolini's 1919 Fascist Party Manifesto, Nazi fascism was already racist. Article Four of the NSDAP programme denied the right of Jews to be considered German. Other articles hinted at racist, biological politics, by calling for the Germans to be strong and healthy.

Hitler became the leader of the movement in 1920 and asserted the importance of his role. This is the so-called authority of the leader: the 'Fuhrerprinzip'.

After a failed coup d'etat (1923), Hitler added to Nazi doctrine through his infamous text, *Mein Kampf* (*My Struggle*). A complex combination of historical factors subsequently led to the Nazi Party's electoral successes and takeover of power in the 1930s. Here, one cannot ignore the period's successive economic crises (1918–1920, 1929) that made Germans vulnerable to extremist politics. The residue of Prussian Nationalism, revolutionary conservatism and long-standing anti-Semitism in a defeated Germany are further themes worthy of consideration when exploring this period.

see also...

Anti-Semitism; Fascism; Nationalism

Nihilism

This term describes the social-political belief that all values are useless and that morality is equally sterile. It is the rejection of everything and the belief in nothing at all. Hardly a political ideology, it is an 'anti-' doctrine. Psychologically speaking, the term also suggests a fatalistic self-destructive character.

There have never been any significant nihilist political parties or governments. That would rather miss the point. Nihilism has however contributed to European art, culture and philosophy. The term originates in literature. It was first used by the nineteenth-century Russian novelist, Turgenev, in his 1861 *Fathers and Sons*. Herein, Turgenev describes those disillusioned Russian liberal reformers as nihilists. Despairingly, they saw destructive change as the only solution for their country. Drawing from fiction, elements in the Russian anti-Tsarist revolutionary tradition subsequently accepted the label to describe their efforts to overthrow the regime. Nihilism is therefore probably best associated with anarchism. Several anarchist writers, horrified at the consequences of liberal democracy and the free market have advocated variations of nihilism. The refusal of nihilists to accept all political and economic doctrines certainly chimes with classic anarchist individualism. Rather differently, on the fringes of the fascist tradition some French and German intellectuals showed a propensity for nihilism during the turmoil of the inter-war years.

After 1945 cultural fashions have sometimes revisited nihilism. Post-modernist thinkers, who tend to reject the stability of all ideas or political perspectives, are sometimes nihilistic in their outlook. Their rejection of the modern period's political and intellectual certainties can be associated with a nihilistic tone. Today, in a society in which capitalist acquisition continues to be a key marker of personal success, many individuals who are unable or unwilling 'to compete in the market' might be drawn to the tradition.

see also...

Post-modernism

Pacifism

Pacifism is the complete opposition to the use of violence and in particular all warfare. The doctrine is also commonly associated with the rejection of national military service on the grounds of personal conscience. Between 1939 and 1945, 59,000 British citizens sought classification as 'conscientious objectors'. The majority were accepted so long as civic war work was adopted instead of direct military service. However, the modern state's response to the refusal to serve in war has not always been so charitable. Desertion and other acts of 'mutiny' have generally been severely punished.

The roots of pacifism lie in ancient Hebrew and Christian theologies. The British pacifist tradition was subsequently perpetuated by the Anabaptists, Quakers and the Plymouth Brethren. In Britain, during the inter-war period, organized Christian pacifism was advocated by the Fellowship of Reconciliation (founded 1914). Complementary British pacifist organizations of that period included the Peace Pledge Union (PPU, founded 1936). In the post-war period the anti-nuclear campaigns of the Campaign Against Nuclear Disarmament (CND) movement continued the tradition which combined Christian morality with socialist internationalism.

Notwithstanding the numerous pacifist leagues and movements that marked twentieth-century Europe, the single most important figure to contribute to pacifism can be found in the anti-imperial doctrine of Mahatma Gandhi (1869–1948). Gandhi opposed all use of violence and instead advocated the use of non-violent resistance to undermine British power in India. Strikes, refusal to pay taxes and disobedience of Courts of Law were all possible peaceful means of furthering the independence movement.

Post-modernism

The world today is sometimes described by commentators as 'post-modern'. What are the origins and meanings of this catchy term? The expression was used for the first time in the precise context of Hispanic literary studies. In the 1930s, Fredrico de Onìs employed the twin expressions 'postmodernismo' and 'ultramodernismo' to account for trends in Spanish modernist literature. At approximately the same time, in Great Britain, the philosopher Arnold Toynbee coined the expression post-modern as a descriptive label for the post-1870 period of European history.

However, the common contemporary usage of 'post-modernism' has its origins in literary, architectural, and philosophical debates of the late 1960s and 1970s. Here, scholars such as Jean-François Lyotard deployed the term to talk about contemporary scientific and cultural developments and to label the present period as distinct from the modernist past. Lyotard's *The Post-Modern Condition* (1979), and subsequent works, outlined the viewpoint that Western intellectual life no longer accepted the key political narratives about itself which had coloured history from at least the Enlightenment onwards. Explanatory philosophies/political ideologies like Marxism were no longer to be taken at face value. In their place post-modern critics discern a mosaic of viewpoints and perspectives in which no political or cultural certainties are available. Now, all ideas and cultural forms are open to constant recycling and playful manipulation. For example, post-modern literature is associated with pastiche, parody and inter-textual referencing. In the wings, there is often a sense of nihilism.

Not all scholars of post-modernism celebrate its arrival. The works of neo-Marxist critics, such as Frederic Jameson, associate the cultural practices of the 1980s and 1990s with the success of liberal free-market economics.

> *see also...*
>
> *Modernism; Nihilism*

Proletariat

This word describes the working class. It is therefore historically rooted in the modern period of industrialization when capitalist investors began to develop methods of mass production associated with the factory. It was in the new industrial factories that a working class developed. Here, men and women worked for little financial reward and were forced to live and work in frequently dangerous conditions. In response, trade union movements gathered workers together to campaign for their defence. Likewise, a working class culture of song, sport, folklore and popular education emerged. Broadly speaking, to repeat, prior to the nineteenth century, in Europe one might describe peasants at work on the land or craftsmen who produced goods in small workshops, but no significant proletariat. Only with industrialization did the new social group of the proletariat emerge.

The development of the working class was not geographically uniform. Thus, for example, in late nineteenth century Italy there was clearly an urban, factory-based, working class culture in the northern industrial cities of Turin or Milan. However, since industrialization had not taken place in the south, there is little sign of a proletariat in that region of the country. A similar picture of variation can be seen across Europe, with those societies such as Britain or Germany, where industrialization was rapidly occurring, having by far the most recognizable groups of proletarians.

Marxist philosophy of history makes the idea of the proletariat a key social group. For Marx, the proletariat would become a revolutionary force. In this perspective it would be the proletariat that brought about the collapse of capitalism and created first socialism and then the utopian communist society. The actual history of the working class has been very different. Industrial production has evolved very differently from how Marx imagined. Notably the notion of being a 'worker' has been slowly replaced by the ever-growing ranks of the middle class.

see also...

Class; Marxism

73

Propaganda

In contemporary history the word propaganda is used to describe political communication. Generally speaking, it is associated with the process of government persuasion in times of war or extreme political polarization. The term frequently also acts as a synonym for political lies and deception. Some of the best-known propaganda has been communicated via the artwork of the political poster. The image of Stanley Kitchener (1850–1916), proclaiming 'Your Country Needs You' to recruit soldiers for the British First World War effort remains a classic image of the twentieth century. However, all forms of communication, from cinema to radio, can serve the purposes of the propagandist.

It would be historically inaccurate to associate propagandizing with any particular political ideology or national government. Like terrorism (i.e. acts of political violence) it is one typical weapon in the armoury of any political group. However, one can begin to make distinctions of scale between the use of propaganda within democratic electoral politics and its place within totalitarian societies such as the Third Reich or the Soviet Union. In a democracy it is accepted that many of the political messages that are presented serve as propaganda. The status of these messages is relatively unimportant. They fill the political arena and compete with many other sources of political information. Sometimes they are believed and therefore taken to be true. On other occasions, they are refuted and thereby denounced as 'propaganda' or 'lies'. This is the very heart of liberal democratic political debate.

Conversely, the role of propaganda in a totalitarian society is very different. Theoretically in this context, all political information is controlled by the state and the dominant political party. Thus, all aspects of communication are organized by the dominant political ideology and its message is constantly circulated without contestation.

Psychoanalysis

Perhaps one of the most enduring images of the twentieth century is that of the psychoanalyst's couch. Here, in repose, the troubled patient talks about his life while the therapist listens and tries to put together an explanation of the neurosis. Psychoanalysis is the theory and therapy of the human mind. Its central lessons were elaborated by Sigmund Freud (1856–1939) while working in Vienna from the 1890s onwards. Many theorists and clinicians have taken up and amended his perspective, among others, his daughter Anna Freud (1895–1982); Carl Gustav Jung (1875–1961); Melanie Klein (1882–1960) and Jacques Lacan (1901–81).

All forms of psychoanalysis (Freudian or post-Freudian) try to explain how and why human beings interact. The central focus is on the individual's unconscious and their processing of childhood development. By exploring the individual's past, their relationship to sexual history and their place within the family, the patient and therapist can discover interpretations which might explain a particular phobia or other mental symptom. Typical is an examination of the patient's feelings in relation to their parents. Unconsciously are they still engaged in a battle to impress their father or to try to challenge his position in relation to the mother? Through gradual reconsideration of what the patient feels to be important about their life, a process of realization and 'coming to terms' occurs. So, central to all psychoanalysis is the idea of identity. Together the patient and therapist strive to reach a comfortable, unproblematic, identity. Or as Freud said: 'to turn hysterical misery into everyday happiness.'

The legacy of Freud's work is enormous. His theories about the mind have given the world concepts such as the 'Oedipus Complex', 'Repression', and the 'Freudian Slip'. From the treatment of illness to advertising, culture and the arts, Freud's view of mankind is commonplace.

Racism

This is usually the belief in the superiority of white Europeans or North Americans over Jews, blacks or subcontinental Indians and other non-white racial groups. The core premise of the doctrine is that racial-cultural distinctions can be made and that they inform a hierarchy of races. Racists are highly élitist and divisive. At the core of racism is a world-view which states that racial separation and mono-ethnic, mono-cultural societies are preferential to race-mixing or 'melting-pot' societies like the United States. To paraphrase further, for a racist multiculturalism cannot function.

In retrospect, the nineteenth and twentieth centuries appear highly marked by racism. As a social-political doctrine the concept of race was notably outlined by the French theorist, Count Alfred de Gobineau in his 1854 *Essay on the Inequality of the Human Races*. Subsequently, social Darwinists applied the theory of evolution to races and to nations. This application of Darwinism further popularized the ideas of racial superiority/inferiority. Nineteenth-century imperialism, West European colonization of Africa and the Far East, was legitimated by racist assumptions. Racism was part of European popular culture and by the turn of the nineteenth century was widely accepted. It is important to underline that as well as scientific legitimation, everyday cultural products, such as newspaper cartoons, carried racially prejudiced stereotypes. Much late nineteenth-century nationalism used ideas of racial superiority in its patriotic rhetoric. By the 1930s Nazi thinking and politics radicalized racism further by applying racial prejudice to pre-existing, mainly religious, anti-Semitism. The final consequence of Nazi policy was genocide.

see also...

Anti-Semitism; Apartheid; Darwinism; Fascism; Multiculturalism; Nationalism; Nazism

Reformation Thought

This term describes the theological doctrines which opposed Catholicism in sixteenth-century Europe and which gave birth to the protestant religion. Reformation thought is associated with the writings and actions of several individuals, notably Martin Luther (1483–1546); Ulrich Zwingli (1484–1531) and John Calvin (1509–64).

Reformation thought challenged the Catholic Church on a number of fundamental issues. For example, the practice of selling 'indulgences' (pieces of paper which allowed the buyer forgiveness for their sins) was disputed by Luther. This German Augustinian monk, a Professor at the University of Wittemburg (Saxony), argued in his '95 theses' (1517) that it was impossible for any power other than God to decide on salvation. His central criticism of the role of the Church heralded the major fissure that became known as the reformation. However, it was by far from the only radical attack on Catholicism in that period. Independent of Luther, Zwingli established a further re-configuration of Catholicism. Going beyond Luther, Zwingli contested the nature of the communion. In orthodox Catholicism the taking of bread and wine was more than a symbolic act. It was a literal process of communing with God. Zwingli refuted this interpretation and argued that the communion was only symbolic. Calvin shared this perspective and developed his own reformation thinking in great detail and clarity. His achievements were in many ways the establishment of protestant doctrine in practice – defining its role in relation to the bodies of the state and society. This process occurred in the Swiss city of Geneva.

Ultimately, the importance of the Reformation remains most critical for practising Catholics and Protestants. For these believers of the opposed Christian faiths the period represents a time of bitter dispute, the birth of a reformed religion or an illegitimate heresy.

Religion

World history has been deeply marked by religion. In short, all religions can be defined by a number of basic elements. Religions are belief systems which place complete faith in God, gods or other transcendental powers. Also central to all religions is the belief that the system of sacred thought can inform daily conduct and human behaviour. Religions provide communities with a focal point; they offer families and individuals a sense of shared values. Institutions such as churches or other meeting points provide both a practical and spiritual site for reflection and communion with God. Notable world religions which have played a major part in historical development include: Christianity (Catholic and Protestant); Judaism; Islam and Buddhism. Despite secularization in Europe, religion continues to play a critical part in world affairs in both the modern and contemporary periods of history.

The work of Emile Durkheim (1858–1917), a father of sociological study, provides one compelling overview of the nature of religion. For Durkheim all religions rested on a key feature. This feature was that religions divided the world into the 'Sacred' and the 'Profane'. The sacred is vital to all religious belief because this is the mystical force which defines the religion and all the elements within it. Conversely, the profane represented the banal and the ordinary. To paraphrase further, at the centre of the sacred-life were symbolic features or literally 'totems'. Exploring primitive aboriginal religion, Durkheim noted that the totem was a symbol of the tribe or social group that believed in the religion. On this basis, Durkheim defined the function of religion in society. He explained that religion was therefore: 'a system of ideas by means of which people represent to themselves the society of which they are members and the opaque but intimate relations they have with it' (1912). Religious worship is therefore a form of community affirmation.

Durkheim's view is, at the very least, exceptionally clever. Here, religions are perpetuated because they provide a self-fulfilling function for the society that believes in them.

The Renaissance

This term is used retrospectively by historians to characterize the intellectual and cultural history of Europe from the late fourteenth century to the sixteenth century, with the early sixteenth century sometimes being further distinguished by the phrase 'High Renaissance'. The expression was first popularized by the nineteenth-century French historian, Jules Michelet (1798–1874). However, it is the writings of his contemporary, Jacob Burkhardt (1818–97), notably his *The Civilisation of the Renaissance in Italy: An Essay* (1860), that did most to establish the concept in the popular imagination. Although a European phenomenon, today we most quickly associate the Renaissance with the art, architecture and scholarship of Italy. Among the best-known examples are iconic pictures such as Leonardo da Vinci's *Mona Lisa*, or the major architectural sites of Florence, Rome and Venice.

So, commonly, the term is used in the study of cultural history to distinguish the clear changes in fashion that were witnessed between the closure of the medieval period and the birth of the modern period. Central issues which were raised during the Renaissance included the development of perspective in painting and the birth of the idea of the individual man as an 'artist' open to commission from the aristocracy and the Church. Likewise, the rise of print technology meant that the ideas of the Renaissance period spread beyond Italy. In this context, the period is associated with the doctrine of humanism. As the literal meaning of the term suggests, the Renaissance was also about man's reflection of himself in historical time. The Italian artists of the period sought a 're-birth' from the Middle ages, or Dark Ages of barbarism, by looking back to classical Greece and Rome. At the heart of the intellectual endeavours of the Renaissance there is a vibrant paradox. On the one hand, creative individuals in the Renaissance held a deep respect for the past, but this was often wedded to a desire for change. This paradox is apparent across Renaissance culture. The glorification of Greek and Roman subjects and styles was central. However, there was also an immense passion to expand human knowledge and to assert progress.

Republicanism

Republicanism is the political support for a particular form of state organization: a republic. A republic, loosely defined, is a state which is governed by its citizens and which does not allow a hereditary leader to establish power. It is therefore the opposite of a monarchy.

Various Republican groups have played significant roles in world history. For example, in the seventeenth century Oliver Cromwell's 'Commonwealth' established a brief period of Republican rule in Britain (1649–60), prior to the restoration of monarchy. In eighteenth-century France, revolutionary movements such as the Jacobins acted to overthrow Louis XVI and establish the First French Republic. Throughout the nineteenth century, political descendants of the original Republicans continued the tradition and the longest and most stable period of Republican governance in France was established in 1870. This, the Third Republic, collapsed only under the pressure of Nazi invasion in 1940.

Republican forces were also critical in the American Revolution and assisted in the framing of the US constitution. The Declaration of Independence (4 July 1776), drafted by Thomas Jefferson (1743–1826) underlined the notion of the need for popular consent for any form of government to be legitimate. Post-civil war, Thomas Paine (1737-1809) represents perhaps the best-known English supporter and theorist of Republicanism. He was active in support of the American and French revolutions. In addition, he added a strong social dimension to the idea of the Republican state by insisting that the state include provision for the poor. This anticipated many features of what was to become the 'welfare state'. Paine's numerous writings include *Common Sense* (1776) and *The Rights of Man* (1792).

see also...

Jacobins

Revolution

World history has witnessed major social upheavals in which complete forms of political authority are violently exchanged for new ones. Classically, this was the case in France in 1789 and subsequently in Russia when the absolutist Tsar Nicholas II was deposed in 1917 to be replaced by the Bolsheviks in the 'October' Revolution later that year. These events and their longer consequences are often described by historians as revolutions. Much historical research and debate focuses on the scale and style of change associated with any given revolution. A classic question posed by historians is whether the 'revolution' was a 'revolution'? What really had changed when one form of government replaced another? Taking a slightly different approach, historical sociologists have offered helpful definitions of the key features of all revolutions. Crudely speaking, revolutions must reflect significant social and political change. One group in power must be clearly replaced by an alternative group. Revolutions are also normally violent. They must represent a sudden break with the past. All revolutions must bring about change which is in some way permanent.

The first standard usage of the word revolution, as a label for a historical event, occurred to describe the English Glorious Revolution of 1688. French revolutionaries in 1789, and after, were also highly aware that they were not simply gaining power but were engaged in a revolutionary period of radical change and reorganization. However, perhaps the nineteenth century is the most significant period in the popularization of the idea of revolution. It was in this era of retrospective analysis of 1789 that Karl Marx (1818–83) developed his socialist philosophy of history in which revolutions play such a central role. Likewise, numerous other historians established the importance of the idea of revolutionary change in French political culture.

> ## see also...
> *Jacobins; Marxism*

The Right and the New Right

This political label originates in the period of the French Revolution. The phrase was used to signify those nobles who sat on the right-hand side of the King in the Estates General (1789). This grouping wished to sustain the monarchy in France and the term continued to be associated with monarchism for much of the nineteenth century. For example, even when Republicanism was firmly established in France by the final years of the century, significant royalist groups advocated a return to one form or another of dynastic governance. In the first part of the twentieth century, the cultural-political group Action Française continued to occupy this space on the political chessboard.

Of course, the phrases 'right-wing' and 'the right' have been adopted across Europe and North America as a synonym for conservatism. The term evokes all of the classic perspectives of this ideological group. Right-wingers are traditionalists, frequently authoritarian and generally opposed to social reform. They are nationalist and imperialist in their outlook. The phrase is therefore an umbrella term which covers an infinite number of conservative figures, movements and parties across the modern world.

On various occasions, political observers have defined 'radical' or 'new' rights. The term 'radical right' is often associated with the development of fascism. Fascism shares many right-wing values but makes a very clear break from conservatism in its call for revolutionary change. This explains the prefix 'radical'. The term 'New' Right has never been systematically defined. It is more often used in a rhetorical flourish to provide a sense of reinvigoration in right-wing thinking. For example, in Britain, the ultra-liberalism of Margaret Thatcher's Conservative Party in the 1970s and 1980s was sometimes described as representing a New Right.

see also...

Conservatism; Fascism; The Left

Romanticism

omanticism describes the international artistic, philosophical and literary 'Romantic Movement' which dominated European cultural life in the late eighteenth and early nineteenth centuries. Well-known romantic figures included the English poets Coleridge (1772–1834), Wordsworth (1770–1850), Byron (1788–1824) and Shelley (1792–1822). In the discipline of the novel, the work of Sir Walter Scott (1771–1832) was equally characteristic. Romanticism was, however, not limited to Britain. In fact its origins lie in the writings of the French philosopher Jean-Jacques Rousseau (1712–78). Importantly, beyond the Rhine, romanticism was also embraced by thinkers and artists such as Schlegel (1767–1845), Goethe (1749–1832) and Schiller (1759–1805).

Given its many different national manifestations the core ideas of romanticism are notoriously difficult to define. This problem was neatly highlighted by the literary scholar J.A. Cuddon who prefaces his own definition of romanticism with the caveat that the term is probably both 'indispensable and useless'. Cuddon also notes that as of 1948, some 11,396 different definitions had already been offered in the literary field! Nevertheless, some core features of the Romantic movement are decipherable. At the heart of many romantic texts is the exploration of mankind's relationship with Nature. This encounter is not interpreted in a rational sense of controlling the natural environment but rather as an exploration of how Nature disturbs man's emotions. A sense of melancholic reflection on the state of mankind was also common to many romantics. The so-called 'Graveyard literature' and the Gothic style were part of the romantic literary experiment. In addition, for romantics the conservative values of moderation and rationalism are to be attacked. In their place there is not only the turbulent world of nature but also the artist's exploration of the inner psyche. In this light, romanticism is sometimes seen as a precursor to the much later birth of Freudian psychoanalysis.

see also...

Psychoanalysis

Rule of Law

Although a rather dry sounding idea, the notion of the 'rule of law' has been central to Western European life. It is on the basis of this notion that civic life remains peaceful, that commerce flourishes and even some aspects of international relations are conducted. Each one of these very different areas is established on the basis of an accepted legal order or system of rules. This is the very meaning of the rule of law. It stands for the idea that in any area of social affairs a legal arbiter can provide a resolution without redress to inter-personal conflict or violence. The system of rules – the law – provides a coherent guideline to temper violence and prohibit anarchic resolutions to conflict. It also offers a kind of level playing field in the regulation of commerce, asserting a set of regulations for issues of contracts, trades or payment.

Legal systems are made by men. They are offered in constitutional documents (e.g.: The American Constitution [1786]; the German Basic Law [1945]); or provided for by legislation, or derived from existing accepted practice and then codified. In some fields theorists of laws have also contributed. The rule of law is especially important to the capitalist liberal democratic state. It is the combination of the law-making legislature, the body of existing law and the judiciary which maintains the system and resolves all matters of dispute. This is true either in Republics such as the United States or in constitutional monarchies like Britain. The constitutions of these states provide a legal guidebook for the practice of government. Additional legal apparatus (the existing laws) offer patterns for the regulation of almost all other areas of life.

It is difficult to imagine a society which does not operate on the basis of the rule of law. Even totalitarian societies maintained the idea of law, albeit in the absence of democracy. However, some pre-industrial societies do not establish order on the basis of written law.

see also...

Liberalism; The State

Science

cience as we know it broadly developed in the long Enlightenment period of the sixteenth and seventeenth centuries. It was in this era that many of the scientific ideas upon which most of our later knowledge is based were first discovered and argued. Among the range of fields which were revolutionized, astronomy remains a good example. Here, the contributions of Copernicus (1473–1543) and Kepler (1571–1630) were ground-breaking. They established the basic principles of the earth's relationship to the sun. This fact alone altered the kind of world in which we live. Similarly, as is well known in the folk-tale of the apple falling from the tree, Sir Isaac Newton (1642–1727) posited his theorization of gravity. Underpinning these and many other smaller scientific shifts, was the rise in a basic confidence to be able to explain the forces of the physical world through observation, theorization, experiment and induction. These are just some of the key aspects of what is sometimes called the 'scientific method'. This rational and 'truth seeking' approach to human-life continues to mark the

Western intellectual world. It stands in marked contrast to either religious belief or neo-pagan forms of physical experimentation which are sometimes colourfully defined as 'magic'. It also stands in contrast to extra-European belief systems, some of which still remain focused on the religious or what we would call the superstitious.

On many occasions the answers which science has offered have come into marked contrast with these other belief systems. Notably, this was the case in the realm of the theory of evolution and the explanation of the creation of the Earth. On both issues, orthodox Christianity challenges science and vice versa. Confidence in scientific method has also been seriously undermined by many of the ways in which scientific discovery has been applied. The fear of science has been commonplace. And, in response to events such as the dropping of the atomic bomb (1945) this is understandable. Today, it seems we live in an ever-increasingly scientific environment, but one which still nevertheless breeds new uncertainties.

Secularization

Secularization is the fall in influence of religion in twentieth-century Europe and, to a lesser extent, around much of the rest of the world. Evidence of such a decline is abundant, especially in Britain. Numerous surveys and opinion polls suggest the ever decreasing importance of sacred beliefs in everyday life. For example, common ethical and moral decisions about lifestyles are increasingly made without reference to religious observance. More and more individuals express reservations about the nature and power of God. Attendance of both Catholic and Protestant Churches has faltered. Since at least 1945 the number of clerics working in the main European Churches has halved. The institution of organized religion has lost authority and is less and less important in the community.

Over much of the century, it has been the policy of most European states to detach their exclusive support for any single religious belief. National education systems do not underpin religious belief systems but instead provide broadly secular introductions to world religions. Likewise, in most cases blasphemous literature is no longer prohibited by the state. These aspects all suggest that secularization has indeed taken place.

Historians and sociologists explain the decline of religion in different ways. They suggest that key features of modern industrialized society are not compatible with a continuation of strong organized religious belief. To paraphrase the explanation further, social fragmentation and the break-up of community structures mean that dominant religions no longer play a central role in life. Other institutions such as the state law, state schools and state hospital services have replaced areas in which the Church was previously important.

see also...

Religion

Separatism

This word describes the process which takes place when one self-defined cultural group wishes to form its own government and thereby to separate from its existing political authority. Separatism is a variation of nationalism.

To elaborate, separatists conclude that their own nation must control its destiny through self-government and in so doing they seek to remove all contact from the previously dominant power. Often this power is a pre-existing nation-state. The term secessionist is sometimes used interchangeably to account for the same phenomenon. Likewise, some scholars have also employed the term 'regionalist' to euphemistically account for regional community challenges against nation-states, usually with the threat of separation waiting in the wings.

A number of separatist movements have been active in Europe in the twentieth century. Perhaps the best-known group are the Basques. They consider that their Basque homeland should not be part of metropolitan Spain. They underline that they have their own language, customs and culture and that therefore they should also have governmental autonomy apart from Madrid. Comparable separatists can be found amongst the Flemish-speaking community in Belgium. Here, in the 1990s particularly, the Vlaams Block group has militated for the separation of the French and Flemish-speaking communities. In Canada, the French-speaking Quebecois nationalists have fought for separation from the English-speaking dominant state. As these examples illustrate 'separatism' is best used in the context of late nationalist movements rather than those of the first period of nationalist expansion in the nineteenth century. Italian nationalism of that early period was irredentist. That is to say it emphasized the promotion of a more general sense of unity rather than a specific break with a centralized regime.

see also...

Federalism; Nation-State; Nationalism

Social Democracy

This political idea is a brand of socialism and it reflects many aspects of this ideological family. Social democrats are egalitarian and hold an optimistic view of the potential of mankind. They are also collectivist. Social democrats believe that societies are best organized through mutual assistance rather than by uncontrolled free economic competition. Social democracy is also internationalist. Its adherents know that social injustices are not limited to a single nation but represent a global challenge.

Despite its origins in the same historical tradition, social democracy differs fundamentally from Marxism. Social democrats, or reformist-evolutionary socialists, do not adhere to Marx's determinist philosophy of history. They do not believe that social equality can be achieved only by a violent proletarian revolution. Instead, reformist socialists are prepared to work within the liberal state to achieve better social provision. Formal rejection of Marxism was announced in the work of another German theorist, Eduard Bernstein (1850–1932). In his work *Evolutionary Socialism* (1898) he argued that democracy meant that social justice could be achieved whilst working with the bourgeois state. The votes of working men meant that violent revolution was no longer necessary. In Britain, where Marxism never gained much popular support, the left-wing has been especially marked by social democracy. Founded in 1900, the Labour Party participated in electoral politics and formed its first full government in 1945. In the initial post-war period, Labour governments attempted to pursue a socialist agenda of nationalization of industry (partial state control of the economy), the creation of the welfare state and the introduction of egalitarian principles to state education. Very minimal redistribution of wealth occurred through taxation and the extent to which results reflected core ambitions remains debatable.

see also...

Marxism; Nationalization; Socialism; Welfare State

Socialism

Socialism developed as a political force in Europe in the nineteenth century. It is a classic political ideology which is comparable to conservatism or liberalism. Its core principle is the reorganization of society on an egalitarian and a co-operative basis. Socialism, like anarchism, is libertarian. Socialists are optimistic about the fundamental nature of mankind. They note that it is the capitalist world that alienates individuals from each other and forces them into futile and damaging competition. If humans were left to co-operate with each other then a greater degree of harmony would be achieved than that which is offered on the basis of individualism. Socialism, generally speaking, is a utopian doctrine that is dedicated to change.

Socialists are also internationalists who believe that people across the world are exploited by similar forces of oppression. All varieties of socialism question the morality of liberal capitalism and the private ownership of property. For socialists the free market provides comfort for some individuals but it fails to provide security, well-being or happiness for the vast majority. Notably the rise of uncontrolled industrialization in the nineteenth century meant that workers, their families and others suffered intense hardship whilst those that owned the factories seemed to experience comfortable, relatively gentle, lives.

Different varieties of socialism have marked world history. Russia was governed by Marxist-Leninist socialism from 1917 to 1989. After 1945, much of Central and Eastern Europe was ruled by Russian imposed socialism. In Western Europe, anti-Marxist, social democracy has achieved some success in tempering capitalism without in anyway damaging its fundamental structures. In China, Maoism offered a further reinterpretation of Marx and Lenin.

see also...

Leninism; Maoism; Marxism; Social Democracy; Stalinism

Sovereignty

Sovereignty is the label given to the complete legal authority of the nation-state. From the sixteenth century onwards a clear sovereign power existed in the form of the monarch. The monarchies of Europe held complete political-legal authority. They were 'sovereign' and the power over their geo-political territories represented their sovereign lands. Outside this area were other sovereign nation-states. Each sovereignty represented a single and distinct legal zone in which other states had no authority. Sovereignty is therefore (a) internal legal power, combined with (b) external mutual respect between sovereign states.

Experiences of sovereignty have varied from one sovereign nation to another. For example, British sovereignty for much of the modern period has resided in Parliament. This is the sovereign legislature in which laws are made and revised based on the voting patterns of the members of the parliament. Much of the sense of parliamentary sovereignty, or independent power, lies in the fact that no parliament is allowed to constrain the terms of reference of the next parliament. Similarly, no other institution within the British nation-state holds political authority over Parliament. These perspectives on sovereignty reflect the relative stability and continuity of British history and the very survival of the parliamentary legislature on which they focus.

Beyond Britain, many other conceptions of sovereignty draw out more complex questions of the nature of authority and power. This is famously evident in the German legal theorist Karl Schmitt's (1888–1986) definition of sovereignty which was offered during the highly unstable years of Weimar government. For Schmitt sovereignty did not reside in a legal network or institution but instead: 'Sovereign is he who decides on the exception.' That is to say ultimate political authority lies in the hands of whoever successfully claims it and then wields it.

see also...

Nation-state

90

Stalinism

Stalinism accounts for the ideological position and practical governance of Russia as conceived by Josef Stalin (1879–1953). As with so many other terms which are explored in this book, Stalinism is a controversial concept which has been interpreted by historians and contemporaries in a variety of different ways. One plausible definition of Stalinism is that it simply describes the action of its originator and his contributions to Russian history. Central characteristics of the Stalinist totalitarian regime, which began by the late 1920s, include the mass industrialization of Soviet society alongside the disastrous attempts to collectivize agricultural production. By 1934 to 1939, Russian society was also marked by Stalin's violent attacks on the Party apparatus and the Army. The 'Purge' destroyed the lives of scores of innocent Russians who were suddenly accused of betraying the Party and the national interest. Ultimately, perhaps Stalin's greatest achievement was to defeat Nazi invasion. However, this had followed the compromise of the Hitler-Stalin Pact (1939–41) which had left Russia ill-prepared for war. On the other hand, when war came the personality cult which Stalin had cultivated since his fiftieth birthday celebration (1929) provided a point of unity for the Russians to rally around.

Although for much of the time Stalin operated as a political pragmatist he constantly claimed to be expanding the theoretical knowledge of Marxism-Leninism. Probably the most important doctrinal contribution to the theory of revolution came in his 1924 essay 'Socialism in One Country'. Counter to Trotsky, this perspective claimed that the development of a Marxist revolution was perfectly possible within Russia alone. The Soviet Union was the vanguard of revolution which would develop no matter what occurred in the Western liberal democracies. It did not need a global proletarian revolution to support its internal development.

see also...

Leninism; Marxism; Trotskyism

The State

This word describes the combined powers of a government's executive and legislature, its bureaucracy, legal mechanisms, the judiciary, the army, the police and its media institutions. Since most of these institutions have only fully expanded in the nineteenth and twentieth centuries, the idea of the state predominantly refers to contemporary history. However, it should be underlined that the beginnings of the state, its philosophical justification and inception, lie much earlier in the writings of Classical Philosophy, the Renaissance and subsequently the Enlightenment period. The concept of the state entered modern political thought at the end of the sixteenth century in, for example, the writings of Botero.

Most contemporary political ideologies (for example, socialism, fascism, conservatism, liberalism) believe in very different roles for the state. For example, in brief, for a liberal the state exists to protect property and economic order. It also acts as a fair judge so as to resolve any issues of dispute. In this case the state should be limited and not hamper economic rights of free trade. Alternatively, for social democrats the state represents the mechanism which provides the means for social improvement. The use of taxation provides a legal mechanism for the redistribution of wealth from the economically strong to the economically weak. These viewpoints are very different again from either the Marxist or the conservative conception of the state. For Marxists the state represents the power interests of the ruling class. It is a source of power which allows the dominant social group to exercise control over the classes that are being exploited. On the other hand, for conservatives the state is perceived as a kind of natural, almost spiritual, adjunct to the national community. This perception is usually known as the 'organic' view of the state.

see also...
Rule of Law

Syndicalism

Syndicalism is a political doctrine which gained some prominence in France, Spain and Italy from the late nineteenth century until at least the 1930s. It was a left-wing movement which argued for social change. However, it was distinct from both classic Marxism and from social democracy. Syndicalists were revolutionaries who argued that social justice was best obtained through the trade union movement. In particular, to paraphrase the syndicalist case, in the aftermath of a revolutionary break with capitalism it would be the unions that took control of industry and the economy. The more typical socialist idea of the state control of production was rejected. This anti-statism has led syndicalism to be closely associated with anarchism. In fact, some commentators have even described this idea as being 'anarcho-syndicalism'. Certainly the movement was influenced by the leading anarchist thinker Joseph Proudhon (1809–65).

Syndicalism is also frequently associated with another French political theorist, Georges Sorel (1847–1923). Sorel is best known for his contribution to political thought made in his book *Reflections on Violence* (1908). This critical work provided syndicalist doctrine with an explanation of how violent revolution could halt capitalism. In it Sorel argued that the idea and pursuit of the General Strike was the best revolutionary device open to the oppressed. The trade unions, to broadly paraphrase Sorel, should glorify and popularize the idea or 'myth' of strike action. This itself would prepare the way for a final complete end to capitalism.

Syndicalism was influential in much of the European trade union movement. However, Sorel's work also became a source of inspiration for the fascist leader Benito Mussolini (1883–1945). Sorel is therefore sometimes analysed as an intellectual precursor to fascism. Without doubt his emphasis on violence and the power of myths and spectacles chimes with developments in the politics of the far right-wing in the 1920s and 1930s.

Technocracy

Technocracy means 'rule by élite technicians'. The phrase and word were first employed in California, USA, by the engineer William Henry Smyth in 1919. Today, it describes any state in which the technological élite, experts and scientists, hold political power. So far in world history, the idea of the technocratic state has remained purely theoretical. Beyond the world of science fiction literature there have been no major working technocracies.

The idea of technocracy has gained most attention in the home of its birth and, also briefly, in France. Smyth's notion of technocratic governance gained some popularity in the face of the 1930s economic depression. During the post-1945 period in Europe, French intellectuals became interested in the role of the expert in governance. It was noted that with industrialization the technocratic élite were gaining increased power. Likewise, the ever closer opinions of the political left and the political right appeared to leave most practical issues of governance in the hands of 'élite' civil servants

who represented a version of technocracy. The French technocratic school found their own theoretical father in the nineteenth-century social thinker, Count Henri de Saint-Simon (1760–1825). Saint-Simon's writings and movement had anticipated and favoured a technocratic society. His 1814 'The Re-Organization of European Society' had called for a Federal government of Europe run by a parliament of intellectual 'experts'. Moreover, in 1819, Saint-Simon famously noted that if France had to choose between its producers, thinkers and artists ('the technocrats') over its princes and wealthy élite, the former group would be the greater loss.

Saint-Simon's influence in nineteenth-century thought was widespread. However, despite one experiment in Saint-Simonian living – an experimental society was briefly established in 1832 in Ménilmontant – his work was limited to intellectual rather than practical influence. This has been the common fate of the technocratic tradition.

Terrorism

This is the use of violence to achieve political ends. Across history there is nothing especially new about the concept, however it is in the twentieth century that terrorism has become a subject of international importance and debate. In this period there have been examples of terrorism deployed from both the right-wing and left-wing extremes of the political spectrum. For example, there was the far right-wing pro-colonial 'Secret Army', or OAS, which in the early 1960s tried to remove Charles de Gaulle (1890–1970) from the Presidency of the French Republic. The 1970s were punctuated by the terrorism of the radical left. For example, there were the Red Brigades in Italy and in Germany there was the 'Baader Meinhof' group.

Terrorism is associated with political movements that form military groups to exert direct pressure on those they are unable to persuade by alternative means. For the terrorist, acts of violence are legitimated by their opponents' use of comparable oppression. Obviously terrorist organizations are clandestine and conspiratorial. In the interests of secrecy they are also usually structured around loosely affiliated cells, with only a few members of the network being aware of the activities of their comrades. They engage in violent attacks against their enemies. Increasingly sophisticated means of destruction are used either to directly assist the political cause or to draw mass media attention to its goals.

In the late twentieth century, national independence or separatist groups were the most common exponents of terrorism. They perceived their use of force as a counter-weight to the official activities of the dominant nation-state or the distant imperial power; its police force and its military. On 11 September 2001 an escalation of terrorism, almost beyond imagination, saw the destruction of the World Trade Center, New York and significant damage to the Pentagon, Washington DC.

see also...

Separatism

Totalitarianism

Totalitarianism is a form of government which prioritizes the interests of the whole (usually, the nation or the political ideology) over the rights of the individual. It is therefore not an ideology in itself but a concept of governance which several different political doctrines have explored or which have been comparatively identified with by academic observers.

The term totalitarianism was first used by the fascist leader Benito Mussolini (1883-1945) to describe his desire for the Italian state to control totally all realms of human activity. Put simply, the fascist government wished to end the distinction between the political world and the social world of the individual. Total states would observe and regulate every aspect of life to fulfil the needs of the nation and its embodiment, the Fascist Party. The citizen of the total state would be expected to be active and to be committed to the collective will.

In the 1950s and 1960s, totalitarianism was analysed by historians and theorists who were opposed to the concept but who wished to better understand its dynamics. A set of common features which underpinned fascist, Nazi and Soviet governments were identified and debated. The following characteristics of totalitarianism are loosely drawn from the famous works of C.J. Friedrich and Z. Brzezinski. To paraphrase, all totalitarian states are based on the power of one ideology's control of the mechanisms of government; they are one-party states and they employ forces of repression to stop opposition. Totalitarianism has existed only in the industrial age and each totalitarian state holds complete control over information and communication, as well as the armed forces. Also, they each control the economy.

Since their heyday, critical theorizations of totalitarianism have declined in popularity.

see also...

Communism; Fascism; Nazism; Stalinism

Trade Unionism

Trade unions are organizations which represent workers' rights. They developed in nineteenth-century Europe to defend the workforce from brutal exploitation. The point of a union is based on the premise that if those employed in an industry need to protect themselves from unfair employer treatment then their resistance is best founded on a collective response. The withdrawal of labour, or 'strike action', is just one way in which unions have brought pressure on employers to change conditions. Classically, unions campaign for improved safety conditions, better wages, shorter working hours and other social rights in the workplace.

Trade unions first developed more strongly in countries where industrialization was most harsh. In Britain the earliest workers' organization was established in the late eighteenth century in the woollen industry. In 1850 a skilled engineers' union was established. Sixteen years later the Trade Union Congress (TUC) was formed to draw together groups from different industries. It became a forum for joint union organization. Critically the establishment of key union rights was further expanded in 1906. The Trades Dispute Act of that year defended unions against legal retaliation by employers. This was a response to the infamous 'Taff Vale' incident in which striking unions had been prosecuted for their actions. As occurred in Britain, France and Germany witnessed significant unionization in the light of industrialization. For example, historians have estimated that more than three and a quarter million Germans were members of unions at the outbreak of war in 1914.

As well as representing their workers through industrial negotiations, the trade union movement realized that political influence was also important to defend the rights of their members. However, the different European unions did not share a common political method.

> **see also...**
> *Syndicalism*

Trotskyism

The term describes the life and political writings of the Russian revolutionary Leon Trotsky (1879–1940, originally named Bronstein). Trotskyism is a variation of Russian Revolutionary Marxism which emerged throughout its creator's lifetime but was especially defined in opposition to the interpretation of Marxism and Russian politics developed after Lenin's death (1924) by Stalin (1879–1953). The term has therefore been used by supporters as well as by opponents as a means of suggesting a deviation from the orthodox Stalinist line. As is well known, Trotsky was ultimately assassinated on Stalin's orders. He was murdered while living in exile in Mexico City.

Trotsky's central contribution to Russian Marxism is the idea of permanent revolution. Adapting Marx, Trotsky argued that in Russia the key revolutionary forces were the workers and the peasants and that these groups, not the bourgeoisie, would overthrow the absolutist Tsar. Thus, unlike the events of the French Revolution (1789), Russia would move rapidly from a democratic revolution to a socialist one. To paraphrase further, this would occur because of support from other socialist revolutions outside of Russia. In addition to this concept of 'permanent revolution', Trotsky later believed in unity between Russian and other European socialist groups. He also identified the growing danger of bureaucracy within the Soviet Union. In Western Europe, he underlined the need again for unity against the growing threat of Fascism in Italy and Germany. This was in strict opposition to Stalin's conception of the revolution being conducted on the basis of 'Socialism in One Country'.

see also...

Marxism; Stalinism

War

The classic political idea of a war is a violent confrontation between two or more sovereign states. For whatever reasons, these states have been unable to resolve their disagreements by the use of diplomacy. One or more of the states might actively have wished to engage in violent dispute, acting in the belief that this was the best way to achieve its objectives. Among the many motives for wars are imperial ambitions, dynastic or territorial disputes, religious or political differences or issues of revenge which date from a previous conflict. Civil wars are distinct from other warfare because they are conducted between peoples living within the same state. Often they have been the most bitter and violent conflicts precisely because they have been conducted on the basis of the breakdown of civil order.

Over the course of history the impact of war has been immensely important. The fear of war, the planning for war, and the pursuit of war have shaped society. For example, feudalism was a social and economic system which to an extent was based on the attempted organization of military affairs in the preparation for war. In the feudal system the king was dependent on his lords to raise a military force. In the modern period the logistics of war have been no less significant than in the past. Governments have invested hugely in arms manufacture and other military related industries. In exchange, the defence industry has provided states with new forms of military capability. These have of course included weaponry of a highly destructive nature. Some commentators, like the American intellectual Noam Chomsky (b.1928), have even argued that this link between commerce and the state has occurred to such a degree that governments are to an extent dependent on the wishes of the arms industry. The sinister phrase 'military-industrial complex' describes this highly disputed concept. It seems that even in times of peace the issue of war haunts mankind.

Welfare State

This term refers to those governments which seek to provide systematic social welfare for their citizens. It is a critical element of social democratic thinking because it is an obvious means by which the state can intervene to provide social equality. Examples of different types of welfare states have existed across the world in the twentieth century. In post-war West Germany the very constitution (the Basic Law) called for the creation of a 'Social State', for example. However, it is the British Welfare State, devised during the Second World War and implemented immediately thereafter, that remains a classic model for how democracies can seek to improve the conditions of their peoples.

The combination of popular sentiment and the practical growth of state intervention in war made reform a possibility in Britain in the 1940s. Wartime planning for military success showed the potential for further collective endeavours to combat social injustice in the post-war era. These aspirations were reflected in literature such as J.B. Priestley's *Out of the People* (1941) or Eleanor Rathbone's *Case for Family Allowances*. On a governmental level the famous *Beveridge Report* (1942) outlined national insurance systems, state health provision, children's allowances and other mechanisms. The election of the first majority Labour Government, under Atlee, in 1945, made this spirit of reform politically possible. Implementation followed in a variety of acts of parliament. Notably these included the National Insurance Act (1946) which created the Ministry of National Insurance, later named the Department of Social Security. The British National Health Service was formed by legislation in 1946. This aimed to provide free patient care for all those in need. State education had already been outlined in the earlier, pre-Labour, Education Act (1944).

see also...

Social Democracy

Zionism

This term was first used in 1892 by Nathan Birnbaum to describe the formation of a Jewish state in Israel. It became the name for the activists who supported this stance. Although not the inventor of the term, the figure who is most associated with the birth of Zionism is the Viennese Jew, Theodore Herzl (1860–1904). His campaigning and writing led to the formation of the First Zionist International (Basel 1897). This served as a rallying point for the disparate Jewish groups from Eastern and Western Europe who were already seeking to settle in Palestine. Further Zionist meetings followed until 1917 when the British Government 'Balfour Declaration' offered Jewish settlement in the British Mandate of Palestine. On 14 May 1948, Palestine was partitioned and the State of Israel declared.

The intellectual origins of Zionism lie in the nineteenth century. In a period of nationalism, in which, for instance, the nation-states of Germany and Italy were first formed, Jewish intellectuals thought of creating a secular homeland. The Judaic theological doctrine of 'The Gathering In of the Exiles' and the 'Rebuilding of Zion' seemed to chime with the epoch of nation building. Moreover, despite progress of civil rights and assimilation many Jews in Europe continued to feel threatened by anti-Semitism. The life of Herzl captured this spirit of the times. In 1896, his pamphlet *Der Judenstaat* [*The Jewish State*] declared that the Jewish Question was one of international importance. His subsequent activities led him into diplomatic relations with all manner of figures who might be able to offer the Jewish peoples statehood. Turning to the British, in 1903 Herzl was offered a Jewish colonial dominion in East Africa. Although initially welcomed, the offer was vehemently opposed by the wider Zionist community. This disagreement points to the many doctrinal factions which constituted Zionist ideology in its formative years.

see also...

Anti-Semitism; Nationalism

Further Reading

The volume of introductory literature which is devoted to the ideas discussed in this short book is enormous. In addition to the general titles listed below, I would like to draw attention to the following useful series and their publishers: Hodder '101 Key Ideas'; Hodder 'For Beginners'; Hodder 'Access to History'; Longman 'Seminar Studies in History'; Icon Books 'For Beginners...'; Open University Press 'Concepts in the Social Sciences'; Oxford University Press 'Very Short Introductions'; Penguin, 'Political Leaders in the Twentieth Century'; and Routledge 'Key Ideas'.

Brogan, H., (1990) *The Penguin History of the United States of America*. London, Penguin.

Bullock, A. and O. Stallybrass (eds) (1977) *The Fontana Dictionary of Modern Thought*. London, Collins.

Cuddon, J.A. (1979) *A Dictionary of Literary Terms*. London, Penguin Books.

Goodwin, B. (1995) *Using Political Ideas*. Chichester, John Wiley and Sons.

Heywood, A. (1998) *Political Ideologies: An Introduction*. Basingstoke, Macmillan.

Imperato, T. (2000) *An Introduction to Early Modern European History 1450-1610*. London, Hodder and Stoughton.

Joll, J. (1990) *Europe since 1870*. London, Penguin.

Laqueur, W. (1992) *Europe in Our Time: A History 1945–1992*. London, Viking.

Mazower, M. (1998) *Dark Continent. Europe's Twentieth Century*. London, Allen Lane.

Palmer, A. (1986) *The Penguin Dictionary of Modern History 1789-1945*. Harmondsworth, Penguin.

Palmowski, J. (1997) *A Dictionary of Twentieth-Century World History*. Oxford, Oxford University Press.

Pearce, M. and G. Stewart, (1992) *British Political History 1867–1995: Democracy and Decline.* London, Routledge.

Scruton, R. (1996) *A Dictionary of Political Thought. Second Edition.* London, Macmillan.

Also available in the series

TY 101 Key Ideas: Astronomy	Jim Breithaupt	0 340 78214 5
TY 101 Key Ideas: Buddhism	Mel Thompson	0 340 78028 2
TY 101 Key Ideas: Business Studies	Neil Denby	0 340 80435 1
TY 101 Key Ideas: Chemistry	Andrew Scott	0 340 80392 4
TY 101 Key Ideas: Ecology	Paul Mitchell	0 340 78209 9
TY 101 Key Ideas: Economics	Keith Brunskill	0 340 80436 X
TY 101 Key Ideas: Evolution	Morton Jenkins	0 340 78210 2
TY 101 Key Ideas: Existentialism	George Myerson	0 340 78152 1
TY 101 Key Ideas: Genetics	Morton Jenkins	0 340 78211 0
TY 101 Key Ideas: Information Technology	Stephen Gorard and Neil Selwyn	0 340 80437 8
TY 101 Key Ideas: Linguistics	Richard Horsey	0 340 78213 7
TY 101 Key Ideas: Literature	Brenda Downes	0 340 84539 2
TY 101 Key Ideas: Philosophy	Paul Oliver	0 340 78029 0
TY 101 Key Ideas: Physics	Jim Breithaupt	0 340 79048 2
TY 101 Key Ideas: Politics	Peter Joyce	0 340 79961 7
TY 101 Key Ideas: Psychology	Dave Robinson	0 340 78155 6
TY 101 Key Ideas: World Religions	Paul Oliver	0 340 79049 0

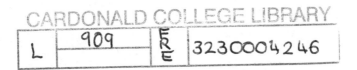